WHERE MURDER LIES

DEATH AND DECEPTION IN WEST HOLLYWOOD

BURL BARER
FRANK C. GIRARDOT JR

WILDBLUE
PRESS

WildBluePress.com

Where Murder Lies published by:
WILDBLUE PRESS
P.O. Box 102440
Denver, Colorado 80250

Publisher Disclaimer: Any opinions, statements of fact or fiction, descriptions, dialogue, and citations found in this book were provided by the author, and are solely those of the author. The publisher makes no claim as to their veracity or accuracy, and assumes no liability for the content.

WILDBLUE PRESS is registered at the U.S. Patent and Trademark Offices.

ISBN 978-1-964730-99-8 Hardcover
ISBN 978-1-970361-00-1 Trade Paperback
ISBN 978-1-964730-98-1 eBook
Cover design © 2025 WildBlue Press. All rights reserved.

Interior Formatting and Book Cover Design by Elijah Toten
www.totencreative.com

WHERE
MURDER LIES

IN MEMORY OF STEVE JACKSON

NOTE

This book is the result of years of research, extensive interviews with primary characters and experts on the topics discussed. Any errors of fact are unintentional. Commentary quotes are, in some instances, reconstructed from conversations and amended for ease of reading and understanding. All photographs are for illustrative and educational purposes only, and their inclusion did not add to the cost of this book.

Frank and I believe that it is important that you understand the social situation of the time and place in which the murder took place, and we have done our best to tell you this story in a simple conversational manner. We hope you will find this story as fascinating, troubling, and compelling as we did. If you have any questions or comments, you may address them to us via our publisher, WildBlue Press.

—Burl Barer

CONTENTS

PROLOGUE

Five days before Christmas 2017, Yelena Itaev sat in front of Judge Fernando Olguin in a non-distinct federal courtroom on the edge of Little Tokyo in downtown Los Angeles.

Yelena, 35, a dark-haired woman with bluish-green eyes and a warm, trustworthy smile, was worried about getting home. She had two children and a dog to take care of.

Her parents, persecuted Jews who had left the former Soviet Republic of Belarus for a better life in the United States, were running out of patience and believed any issue Yelena had with the court, or the U.S. government, could be settled today.

Maybe they would celebrate. It would be the final night of Hanukkah, a time traditionally celebrated with the lighting of the menorah's last candle—a reminder of the miracle of the Jewish holiday.

It would be a miracle if Federal District Judge Fernando Olguin accepted a plea deal worked out between Yelena and federal prosecutors in the Central District of California, which includes Los Angeles.

Yelena's attorney explained his client's predicament: she was a dutiful wife caught up in a scheme hatched by her husband, Mark Itaev.

"Ms. Itaev's involvement in the case was essentially depositing fraudulent checks in the bank on four occasions," explained her attorney. "This was done at the direction of her husband, Mark Itaev."

Her lawyer explained that out of loyalty to her husband and religious marital custom, she couldn't refuse to participate in these crimes over which she now felt shame and remorse.

"In retrospect, she would never have done that; but at the time, she agreed to do it, and it was unfortunate that she felt in that position not to be able to refuse the demands of her husband."

He also pointed out that the dutiful and obedient wife had no prior criminal record.

"She's been a law-abiding citizen. She's grateful for the opportunity that she's had coming to the United States after having a difficult childhood in Russia."

The judge couldn't hear the prosecutor roll his eyes, but he knew the facts of the case: Between 2012 and 2013, Yelena and Mark Itaev, along with two other men, engaged in a bank fraud scheme targeting Bank of America.

The scam involved getting ahold of stolen checks, which were then altered to appear payable to their friends, Dmitri Kocharian and Mark Vincent Norman.

The people who wrote the checks never met Dmitri or Mark Vincent. In fact, they didn't even know the two men. That's because the checks were stolen from mailboxes around Los Angeles and then deposited in a Bank of America via ATM.

Yelena not only deposited bad checks, but she also used a debit card linked to the fraud for a shopping spree at Nordstrom Rack, Broadway Shoes, and CVS.

According to the prosecution, Yelena was no innocent, obedient bride.

"She knew what she was doing," Assistant U.S. Attorney Kathy Yu said to Judge Fernando M. Olguin. "And she got a tangible benefit out of it."

The defense attorney, however, came armed with enough well-orchestrated appeals for leniency, and assurances of law-abiding future behavior, to pluck at the heartstrings of an empathetic judge.

Born in Belarus at the apex of the Cold War in 1981, Yelena and her family came to the United States in 1991, just as the Soviet Union was breaking up.

As a child, Yelena suffered from persistent skin problems, leading to constant teasing and ridicule at school.

Doctors in Belarus were unable to effectively treat her condition. Their daughter's dermatological distress, coupled with the blatant anti-Semitism endemic to Russian culture and State television broadcasts, added to the parents' desire for a better life for themselves and their daughter, and assured that Yelena's family's migration from the former Soviet Union to Los Angeles, California wasn't a rash decision.

Upon arrival in Los Angeles, Yelena was treated by the city's top dermatologists. She attended Fairfax High School and then L.A. City College, where she met Mark, a big, handsome guy who wore mostly black and had a proclivity for designer shirts and sweaters that proclaimed "BOSS" or "HUSTLER."

Mark spoke Russian. He was a Jew and understood her culture and the world she came from. Married to Mark, Yelena manifested all of the subservient characteristics of a dutiful Old World bride.

Defense attorney Lichtman continued his alternately heartwarming and heart-wrenching story worthy of classic tales of Jewish folklore.

"There's a letter from Rabbi Bryski who has talked about the effect of a separation of a mother and a young child that could have devastating effects on a child," said the moist-eyed attorney before producing other signed documents from Yelena's employer and her loving parents.

"The employer, Mr. Wilson, says that she's an integral part of the work source center where she works, and she's eager to do additional work," the attorney informed the court before providing written assurances from her parents that Yelena would reform, apologize, and continue through the rest of her life as the honest woman she had always been.

"They talk about her ability to learn from her mistakes; that she's a mature and caring person, reliable, honest, and willing to help others."

As for the defendant herself, "She is remorseful; accepts full responsibility for her criminal acts and vows never to do it again. She is working with the rabbi to stay on the path of being law-abiding, honest, and be a positive role model for her daughters. "

Despite Prosecutor Yu's disdainful objections, ultimately the government played nice.

Yelena pled guilty to one count of bank fraud. She faced 30 years in federal prison and a fine of as much as $1 million, but in return for the plea, she was sentenced to probation and a $15,000 restitution fine.

Judge Olguin sent the young woman home to a family celebration and the lighting of the menorah.

Her husband wasn't so lucky. Mark was sentenced to 44 months in federal prison and nearly $100,000 in fines.

The media never covered the case. It was never on the TV news; it was never written about in the newspaper. That is not to say the story went completely unnoticed. About eight years after that last candle was lit, a young man named Jimmy Kitlas found the tale instructive.

He knew Mark Itaev well, and he even once had a crush on Yelena, but Jimmy's memories of Mark were more closely tied to events involving himself and his then pregnant girlfriend, Audrey Lane.

"In fact," recalls Jimmy Kitlas, "there was one night back in 2004 when Mark, Audrey, and I were all arrested for murder."

THE DEAD BODY ON THE BED

The bent horizontal blinds in the window on the first floor of 921 Sierra Bonita Avenue in West Hollywood made it obvious someone did a lot of peeping out on the neighborhood. Perhaps it was the guy who lived there, or maybe it was the person who killed him.

The guy who lived and died there was Aleksandr Bentsionovich Markzitser. Known alternately as Sasha or Aleks, Aleksandr Markzitser was a pasty, balding, middle-aged former schoolteacher who had come to the U.S. from Russia sometime about a decade earlier.

Despite having lived in Southern California, Markzitser, 44, had the appearance of someone who had never seen the sun.

Now he was dead. Like a character straight out of 19th-century Russian fiction by Gogol, Dostoyevsky, or Kafka, Aleks, aka Sasha, aka Alexi, wasn't an important person, and he wasn't mourned.

In fact, Markzitser's June 8, 2004, murder rated less than a paragraph in *The Los Angeles Times*'s online Homicide Report.

Despite being remarkably strange, the murder wasn't strange enough to garner any media coverage. Then again, babies found in dumpsters and prostitutes set on fire are such mundane occurrences in Hollywood that they seldom make the television news or rate more than a paragraph in *The L.A. Times.*

The crime scene was, at first glance, only mildly peculiar. Markzitser lay fully clothed on a freshly made bed. He might have been napping.

The only sign of violence was at the bedroom door. Locked from the inside, the door had been forced open by sufficient violence to wrench the exterior doorknob almost completely free.

The body was still warm when sheriff's deputies from the nearby West Hollywood Sheriff's Station arrived.

They had been tipped off by a phone call directing them to the apartment. The caller promised that a murder had been committed. The caller also let detectives know where to find Aleks's alleged killer.

An autopsy later determined that Aleks had been strangled.to death—an intentional and intimate method of murder.

Other than that, it was an unremarkable homicide, the type of case detectives relish, knowing they won't have to stay out late solving a murder.

Within hours of getting the call, the case was chalked up as solved and the deputies celebrated the fact that down the road, they would pick up some overtime money testifying in court.

No one except a woman named Kelley Leigh bothered to dig any deeper. She wasn't so sure Aleks's slaying was a mundane event.

"Only three other people were in Aleks's apartment that night," Kelley said later. "There was a couple of barely legal street teens, Patrick James Kitlas and his pregnant girlfriend, Audrey Lane, and a low-level Russian gangster, Mark Itaev."

Leigh knew it had to be one of those three who called the cops.

But knowing who was there didn't explain why they were there, or why Aleks had to die, or why the cops were so quickly called.

It was Mark Itaev who picked up the dead man's cordless telephone and placed the first phone call, declaring the death of Markzitser a murder before cutting the phone lines.

A night shift watch sergeant working the desk at the West Hollywood Sheriff's Substation took the call informing him that there had been a murder at 921 Sierra Bonita, where to find the body, and where to find the suspects.

The deputy's ears perked up when it was explained what Mark Itaev was doing in the dead man's apartment and why he was using the dead man's phone. It was an important tidbit never shared with the press nor the public.

Because the local media didn't take much notice of poor Aleks's demise, the public had no reason to wonder about what they never heard about in the first place.

"The suppression of that information was intentional and strongly enforced," commented Kelley Leigh. "If you suggested revealing it, you were silenced by threats or actual professional punishment. In other words: 'Look the other way. There is nothing to see here.' Nonsense. There is plenty to see here. Your mission, should you choose to accept it…"

Kelley Leigh believed the story needed a deeper investigation. She instictively suspected it was a true crime story unlike most. And, she believed when told, the story would expose layer upon layer of fraud, deception, trickery, lies, and corruption.

In short, she knew that it was one hell of a true crime story.

All murders require three things: motive, means, and opportunity. What was the motive for killing Aleks? Was it preplanned or suddenly situational?

In his book *Practical Homicide Investigation*, retired NYPD Lt. Cmdr. Vernon J. Geberth describes the task investigators have before them when arriving at the scene of a murder and needing to understand, "what has occurred?"

He suggests the question can only be answered after professional and medical evaluation of the "bits and pieces of evidence gathered by the criminal investigator." He goes on to identify those "bits and pieces" as evidence at the scene, statements from the suspects, eyewitness accounts, and autopsy results.

The more Kelley looked at the bits and pieces, the more fascinated she became, and at every point in the story, something new was revealed, someone who had been silent decided to talk, or someone who was afraid to tell the truth in 2004 had the nerve to come clean 20 years later.

As Geberth points out, the first thing you should acquire is a more comprehensive view of the crime scene. It isn't simply the specific address of Aleks's apartment.

WeHo

Located midway between Santa Monica Boulevard to the north and Melrose Avenue to the south, 921 Sierra Bonita is pretty much like any other multi-family dwelling in a middle-class L.A. neighborhood.

The jaundice-yellow stucco, flattish roof, and contrasting eaves painted the color of raw sewage blend in with the building next door, the one across the street, and buildings all over the sprawling west side, the San Fernando Valley, the San Gabriel Valley, or Los Feliz and Highland Park.

Whatever you call it, 921 Sierra Bonita has seen its share of tenants and color schemes. A decade ago, it was pink with white trim. For a while, the building was seafoam green.

The length of Sierra Bonita is a ribbon of cracked sidewalk separating a sandy dirt patch spotted with drought-resistant greenery, discarded furniture, No Parking signs, and weedy, untrimmed trees.

If 921 stands out at all, it is because of an odd pair of white picket fences that enclose a couple fruit trees out front. The trees seem to provide shade for the occupants of the first-floor mid-century monument to a certain brand of California lifestyle: the brand that begins with bad choices and ends on a street in West Hollywood, where parking is impossible and residents, who call their neighborhood "WeHo," worry about encounters with errant *vatos* from 18th Street or vagrants looking for a handout.

Before it officially incorporated in 1984, West Hollywood was just another formless and lawless Los Angeles County neighborhood patrolled by the Sheriff's Department. That meant no LAPD patrolling the streets and bashing heads, no crazy zoning laws, no vice stings, and no big city politics to screw up a good time. A well placed $100 bill could make a lot of trouble disappear.

In the '80s, the HIV/AIDS epidemic barely changed people's behaviors, and West Hollywood was "Boys' Town."

Up on Santa Monica Boulevard, leather-clad young men strolled the sidewalk after dark, waiting for a cash-paying meet-up with a closeted suit from one of L.A.'s family-friendly suburbs.

At clubs like Rage, men dressed in BDSM gear or like the Village People. They popped amyl nitrate, snorted coke, slammed crank, and downed champagne like rock stars under a pink-and-purple neon sky.

Before Boys' Town, West Hollywood, which is about two miles from Hollywood proper and its famous sign, was a hippy hangout.

Geographically located along the Sunset Strip, a piece of Sunset Boulevard know for night clubs, rock-and-roll palaces, and fine dining options, the Strip was gang turf run by prolific mobster Meir "Mickey" Cohen, a tough former boxer and one-of-a-kind L.A. mafioso who controlled most of the illegal gambling, dope, and prostitution in West Hollywood by paying off the sheriff's department, the newspaper, and anyone else in a position of power with their hand out.

Cohen's front was a haberdashery on Sunset at a five-points intersection where Holloway and Palm meet the legendary Strip. It is just a few blocks from where Markzitser was killed.

Unlike Aleks, Cohen led a charmed life.

When his friend "Hooky" Rothman was shot to death in the front room of the clothing store, Mickey escaped scrutiny by telling homicide cops he was in the bathroom washing his hands at the time of the murder.

A couple years before that, Cohen beat the rap after shooting a pal named Maxie Sherman. He claimed it was self-defense.

West Hollywood was always an organized crime playground. And the night Aleksandr Markzitser died in his apartment at 921 Sierra Bonita, gangsters were still around, but not like before.

Many old-timers had been transferred from cocktail lounges to prison bars, and there was a new, ever-growing group of newcomers in the shadows of WeHo: homeless youth.

Between 1998 and 2005, Hollywood was defined by three realities: gangs, , crime, and homeless kids.

By 2004, there were as many as 8,000 homeless youths on the streets of Los Angeles County. Most of them roamed the boulevards linking Hollywood with its tourist attractions and boarded-up buildings, and West Hollywood, where things were pricier and slightly more upscale, but safer, less exposed.

"It was like an urban version of *Animal Planet* with mutual destruction," one former street denizen recalled, laughing at her own joke.

"I wish it were that funny," said Frank J. Hagan, a former television producer for *The Oprah Winfrey Show* and *The Phil Donahue Show*, where he first addressed male prostitution as survival sex for young boys in Hollywood.

"Kids come here for several reasons. Hollywood's name evokes warmth, entertainment, and childhood memories—a fantasy of comfort, adventure, and riches. In reality, every kid stepping off a Greyhound bus in Hollywood is prey for social vultures who don't wait for them to hit rock bottom—they're already circling."

Hagan, who also served as a media coordinator for a presidential commission during the Reagan administration's early AIDS crisis, highlighted the overlooked toll of the epidemic.

"The death toll among Hollywood street kids from AIDS is rarely mentioned," Hagan lamented. "Survival sex was killing them instead of sustaining them. They even monetized the risk of death, charging more for unprotected sex, as if the extra cash could ward off disease."

Hagan expressed empathy for youth rejected by their families over gender identity or sexual orientation.

"More kids die from an overdose of religious fundamentalism than from illicit drugs," Hagan said, critiquing toxic parenting that equates emotional abuse with so-called "tough love."

Considering the idea decades later, Kelley Leigh had her own take.

"That whole tough love thing is nonsense," she said. "True love is compassionate and merciful. The Torah says God favors the outcasts—widows, orphans, and strangers. You won't find a group more marginalized than the disillusioned runaways on Hollywood's streets, and the two homeless teens who were in Aleks's apartment the night he was murdered—Jimmy and Audrey—are perfect examples. Believe me, neither of them ever wanted to spend the night on the street."

The existing Los Angeles Municipal Code in 2004 made it a criminal offense to sit, lie, or sleep on a public sidewalk anywhere in the city. This law was created using the flawed logic that if you make something against the law, it won't happen.

That meant Jimmy and Audrey could be arrested if they couldn't find a place to sleep indoors.

"As long as there is no option of sleeping indoors," Judge Marsha S. Berzon argued more than a decade later, "the government cannot criminalize indigent, homeless people for sleeping outdoors, on public property, on the false premise they had a choice in the matter."

Jimmy and Audrey, in 2004, were subject to the laws as they were at the time, and many abandoned buildings used by homeless youths had been boarded up, fenced off, or turned into offices, apartments, hip restaurants, or night clubs as investors gentrified the once run-down neighborhoods.

There were also more police and private security guards patrolling the streets and cracking down on panhandling and loitering. Loitering is the act of lingering in a private or public place for no apparent reason. If you have a reason such as waiting for someone, you aren't actually loitering, even if it may appear that way to someone else.

While hanging around a place for no apparent reason isn't a crime, doing so with the *intent* of committing a crime is illegal. It is the intent that is against the law.

Anti-loitering laws were declared unconstitutional in 1999 for two reasons: they violate the right of free assembly, and they're essentially laws against what someone decides you might be thinking.

Presumption of criminal intent violates presumption of innocence. Despite the rulings against loitering laws, police pretend they still exist.

"Reality is reality," Kelley Leigh said. "A young woman such as seventeen-year-old Audrey Lane, alone at three a.m. on Sunset Boulevard in West Hollywood would be easy prey for sexual predators. In those days, twenty dollars was sufficient legal tender to procure the barely legal. She was lucky to not be alone and to have a kind protector like Jimmy."

Leigh, who was in her late 20s at the time and, by her own admission, an "unlicensed pharmaceutical supplier" with six arrests for selling marijuana, observed Audrey from a distance.

Jimmy, on the other hand, had attached himself to Kelley as a mother figure shortly after arriving in Hollywood. She, in return, did her best to protect and nurture him.

That need for attachment opened the door for others to come into Jimmy and Audrey's inner circle.

Mark Itaev was one of them. He knew plenty of the street kids by sight, if not by name, and often was seen lending a helping hand to various lost children by providing a hot meal and cool sheets in a cheap motel.

To avoid getting in trouble with the police in the spring of 2004, Jimmy and Audrey hung out in an internet café on Sunset Boulevard.

The internet café phenomenon was a thing of its era that fit the bill as a place to stay and not be bothered by the cops for loitering.

Many were open until four or five o'clock a.m., with no age restrictions. For $2.00 an hour, a teen could rent a booth with a high-powered computer and play violent shoot-em-up games like *Counter Strike*, *War Craft*, or *Battle Realms*.

Often, virtual battles spilled out into the streets and in 2002 and 2003, several shootings and stabbings were reported at internet cafés around Los Angeles and Orange Counties.

The fad became such a problem that lawmakers moved in and did what they often do best: created laws designed to rein in the violence and choke out the businesses that were its breeding ground.

Mark, as familiar with the West Hollywood scene as anyone, knew he could find Jimmy at the café when he needed him.

Some might call Mark's actions benevolent. Others have a different take.

"Maybe that seems symptomatic of benevolence to you," said a former Hollywood teen runaway. "To me it always seemed more like grooming—you know, the way a predator grooms victims. They feed you till they have you eating out of their hands. There are many forms of abuse and sometimes it is prefaced by illusions of care and protection.

"I met Mark before I met Audrey."

HOLLYWOOD BOULEVARD

In Los Angeles, homeless teens have little support and few resources.

In 2004 to 2005, approximately 41,329 people experienced unsheltered homelessness in Los Angeles City, with about 10,000 shelter beds available.[1] More than half were reserved for families with children, leaving just over 4,000 for single adults, who formed much of the homeless population. Unaccompanied homeless children, lacking parental or adult supervision, were often overlooked.

My Friend's Place is a youth homeless shelter with a headquarters building on Hollywood Boulevard, just off the Hollywood Freeway. It is tucked into a row of not-so-glamorous businesses, including a self-serve car wash, a storage facility, and a newer Tommy's Burger.

In 1994, this intersection was hit hard by the Northridge earthquake and lost much of its unique charm when it was rebuilt.

A decade later, if the ubiquitous Hollywood sign wasn't so visible in the hills rising above the seedy boulevard, Hollywood proper would be undistinguishable from hundreds of other Southern California neighborhoods.

Jimmy was lucky that a girl he knew from high school recognized him on the street and invited him to come in,

1. Los Angeles Homeless Services Authority (LAHSA) 2005 Greater Los Angeles Homeless Count.

hang out, get his bearings, take a shower, and meet other teens in his situation.

"You know, I got someone who you may be able to hook up with," she told Jimmy. "He might be able to help you earn some money."

The next night, she introduced Jimmy to Mark Itaev.

Jimmy remembered feeling elated.

"I saw this big, imposing guy and when he talked to me, he was kind of imprinted on the me like an alpha dog would imprint on a puppy and I'm like, okay. So, with this guy I can be safe."

Through the grapevine, Jimmy heard that Mark might be connected to a Russian organized crime group operating in West Hollywood. So what? Lots of people say and do lots of things.

Mark was of average height, "but he was a big guy," Jimmy recalled. "Lotta fat, Lotta muscle. He was a big, imposing figure."

His hair was dark and always kind of greasy. Mark, who had a pierced ear, wasn't well-groomed, but he wasn't unkempt either. His hair was longish, but not past the collar. Sometimes he would cut it short depending on the look he was going for at any particular moment.

To Jimmy and others, it also seêmed that Mark, who was "pasty white and kind of greasy" had a perpetual five o'clock shadow. He was always well-attired, , usually dressed in designer clothes, and slicked his hair back with a product that looked like Brylcreem.

Jimmy said he didn't remember Mark's eye color (they're brown) or if he had any tattoos (he doesn't).

"I didn't look him in the eye much. Or anyone else," he recalled. "I have a problem with eye contact. There's something off-putting to it for me."

When Mark spoke, he commanded attention. He would walk into a room and often pause to look around, as if seeking to understand if there was danger ahead.

"Mark looked like a Russian mobster," Jimmy said.

Mark *was* a Russian mobster.

In fact, the Itaev family name was well established in Russian organized crime, and California State law enforcement authorities had been monitoring Russian groups operating in Los Angeles and Hollywood since the early 1990s.

In the early 2000s, they were involved in a wide range of criminal activities, from extortion and narcotics trafficking to sophisticated fraud schemes.

One such scheme that caught the eye of law enforcement was a "daisy chain" tax scam that involved creating dummy companies and forging documents to sell untaxed fuel as tax-paid, resulting in the theft of federal and state excise taxes from the government.

This form of fuel fraud was a particularly lucrative enterprise for Russian organized crime in Southern California.

A decade before Jimmy met Mark Itaev, Mark's uncle Meir "Mike" Itaev was arrested in connection with a "daisy chain" tax fraud scheme that allegedly earned millions before it was shut down by federal authorities.

As for Mark, he had his own grifts: check washing and identity theft. Jimmy wasn't drawn to criminality, but he was assuredly attracted to the lifestyle Mark represented. It was a world away from where he came from.

Everybody comes to Hollywood from somewhere. Jimmy, whose full name is Patrick James Kitlas, nickname Shadow, came to Hollywood on the bus from Riverside Juvenile Hall. And according to him, it wasn't his idea at all.

JIMMY

Jimmy earned the nickname "Shadow" because his manner was so unassuming and childlike that he was almost invisible compared to the assertive and controlling personalities of his contemporaries on the streets.

"He was emotionally like a little kid," Kelley Leigh recalled. "He was easily frightened by any thought of violence, kind, courteous, and eager to please. He couldn't concentrate on any one task for more than a few minutes or moments, but he was remarkably obedient and helpful. He was just the kind of kid who could be used and abused by people with no moral compass."

From age six until high school graduation, Kitlas lived mostly, but not always, with his grandparents on their ranch in Lake Elsinore, California, about 80 miles southeast of Hollywood.

Located in southwestern Riverside County, Lake Elsinore in the 1990s and early 2000s was a haven of competing interests.

The community was still far enough off the beaten path that anyone with a passing knowledge of chemistry and a few cheap implements could cook up a batch of meth and not worry too much about disturbing the neighbors with the smell.

Chances are the chemical odor of a batch being brewed was as enticing to some neighbors as the smell of frying bacon on a lazy weekend morning would be to a non-addict. Hell, a close neighbor might even drop by to borrow a cup of Red Devil lye, a handful of ephedrine, or a measure of any one of the other toxic ingredients it takes to make a halfway decent batch of speed.

Even though it's relatively close to Los Angeles, Southwest Riverside County was fairly removed from being a big city suburb, even in the early 2000s.

Some communities offered relief from the big city. Those popped up among desert brush as a patchwork of up-and-coming housing developments promising parks, decent schools, and low crime.

Nonetheless, those developments sat among rundown truck farms, storefront revival churches, and roadhouses that served booze well after closing time.

Down one road, you might encounter a llama farm; down another, maybe you would find a chicken ranch selling fresh eggs, a small winery, or some artisan with homemade cheese.

You could just as easily run into a meth lab protected by Rottweilers, razor wire, and automatic weapons.

The winding state highway through the national forest drew a collection of biker gangs to the region. The forest, itself more of a desert, made a good hideout for scofflaws, outlaws, and survivalists.

Mega churches also dotted the landscape, attracting cultish conservative Protestants running away from L.A. and its suburbs as they became more culturally diversified and less like Disneyland's idyllic but fake Main Street, U.S.A.

Among those who called Lake Elsinore home were James and Polina Sackett, the grandparents of Patrick James "Jimmy" Kitlas.

The couple and the boy's mother called a ranch on the outskirts of town home. An old homestead, the ranch sits on a piece of property along the Ortega Highway, a treacherous spot of road leading out of Lake Elsinore to Orange County.

It is near a country store and across the highway from a biker hangout known as "Hell's Kitchen." A message board outside the bar reads "I have eHarmony to thank for hooking me up with Jack Daniels."

As a baby, Jimmy was known as Patrick, his birth name.

He was born January 25, 1985, to Paul Kitlas and Priscilla Sackett Kitlas at the Martin Luther Hospital Center in Orange County.

Paul and Priscilla's bliss didn't last long, however, and the couple soon split.

"When Patrick was born, our daughter Priscilla was an eighteen-year-old and an unwed mother. Patrick and Priscilla returned home from the hospital to live with my wife Polena and myself at our ranch in the Cleveland National Forest near Lake Elsinore," Patrick's grandfather recalled.

"Priscilla moved to Santa Ana to go to school and work. [At that time] Priscilla lived with Polena's mother and father in Santa Ana. During that time, Patrick became very attached to us and, of course, us to him. While living in Santa Ana, Priscilla met Billy Wakefield and married. Billy soon joined the Navy and was off to Guam with Priscilla, where he would be stationed for some time."

Jimmy has his own version of his story.

"I was born and that, that was the beginning. That's when my trouble started right about there. And my birth mother gave me up and she tried to keep her boyfriend at the time around by giving me his last name.

"Which is why I have a name Kitlas. My last name isn't Kitlas, it isn't actually attached to my family. Kitlas was the guy who was dating my mom at the time of my birth.

"My birth dad is some random Indian that she got jiggy with. So, she tried to keep this guy around by giving me his name, which naturally backfired, freaked him out and he ran, and I'm trapped with a name it means nothing."

Jimmy's childhood, when he was with his grandparents, was idyllic. When he was with his mother, things were rough.

"From the age of zero until I was about four, I didn't know that my grandparents were my grandparents. I thought they were my mom and dad. And nobody ever told me different. In the quiet, traditional household of my Indian [Native American] grandparents, life was steady, filled with soft conversations, emotional support, and spiritual warmth, though not much physical affection.

"They didn't yell or raise their voices, a stark contrast to what was to come. I was blissfully unaware of my birth mother, Priscilla, or the man she married, Billy, until they stormed into my life and took me away. We moved to Guam, where Billy was stationed, and everything changed.

"Back in those days, Billy and Priscilla were drunks and they were just beating the hell out of each other. Their home was chaos, a terrifying new environment for a child raised in calm.

"When I tried to intervene, to stop their fights, they would both turn on me, and I would just get the dog shit beat out of me. I was thrown into corners, locked in the trunk of a car, and, worst of all, molested by Billy. The abuse was relentless, and when it became too much, Billy planned to send me to an Indian boarding school—a place notorious for its harsh conditions.

"My grandparents, whom I still called Mom and Dad, wouldn't stand for it. They flew from California to Hawaii to Guam to rescue me, determined not to let me endure that fate. My grandmother, a survivor of an Indian school herself, knew the horrors of such places, and my grandfather, a half-breed who escaped that fate, stood by her.

"But something had changed in me. For the year or two I was with Priscilla and Billy, I became terrified of everything: chickens, horses, dogs, even the dark. Before,

I'd wander into the mountains at night without care but now, fear consumed me.

"That fed into a real broken heart. Back with my grandparents, I started acting out at school, desperate for attention. I felt that if I wasn't the center of attention, I wasn't loved. I was going to be rejected. I was going to be sent away. I didn't understand these feelings at the time; I just knew I was scared.

"When I was seven or eight, Priscilla and Billy came for me again. This time, we lived in Washington, and their drinking and fighting hadn't stopped. Now they had my baby brother, and the abuse extended to both of us.

"They were just beating the fucking shit out of me and doing all kinds of horrible shit to me and my brother. Billy continued his assaults when Priscilla wasn't around. Once again, they threatened to send me to an Indian boarding school.

"By the time I returned to my grandparents at nine, I was more aware of my surroundings and felt the pain deeply. I was a fucked-up kid, breaking things, being disrespectful, acting out because I was terrified of rejection."

Jimmy attempted to fit in and in high school in Lake Elsinore, he competed in wrestling and was on the football team. School administrators saw a troubled kid.

"In high school, I was placed in special education classes because they thought something was wrong with me. And there was. I was a very traumatized child. My resentment grew. I started to hate my grandparents, believing they only came for me because they had to, not because they wanted to. This deep sense of rejection led to self-mutilation by eleven, twelve, thirteen, and suicide attempts by twelve and thirteen.

"When Priscilla and Billy took me again, it lasted only a month. I was too big, too strong for Billy to continue the sexual abuse, but goddamn if they didn't beat the dog shit out of me.

"By thirteen or fourteen, I was in my worst spot—loud, defiant, a terrible child. My grandparents, unable to handle a severely injured kid, called the sheriff when I was fifteen. They sent me to group homes, but I ran away, hopping a freight train to Dallas, Texas.

"Life on the streets was rough, and after trouble with some locals, I called the only people I could ever trust, my dad. He bought me a bus ticket from Dallas back to the ranch in California. But I was still a fucked-up kid, still acting out. Eventually, they sent me away again.

"By seventeen, I was a storm of pain and rebellion, carrying the weight of a childhood shattered by abuse, rejection, and fear. My grandparents' love had saved me time and again, but the scars ran deep, and the road ahead was uncertain."

Kitlas's grandmother Polina gave her version of Jimmy's childhood in a written statement. Like many in the family, she referred to Jimmy as Patrick.

"At age 6, Patrick and his mother and stepfather were living in Washington state. Patrick was having trouble in school with self-control. He was evaluated by doctors that advised his parents he had ADD—attention deficit disorder. Pricilla and Billy were overwhelmed, and Polena and I agreed to take Patrick back and raise him..."

Jimmy said ADD was the least of his problems.

"I wasn't disruptive, oppositional, and a 'problem child' because I had a short attention span," he said. "You must understand that I went back and forth between two different worlds. The wonderful world of my grandparents was infused with a calm, loving, gentle spirituality springing naturally from the Native American culture. The world of Priscilla was not the least infused with calm spirituality. The atmosphere was choked by a thick alcohol fog and repeated episodes of abuse that she either didn't know about or knew and ignored."

Jimmy kept a lot of the abuse to himself.

"It was clear that he had self-control issues," his grandfather would later recall. "The school put Patrick in a Special Education program that provided a psychologist to see him two times a week."

Even after that, "Patrick was still having trouble controlling himself in class."

"I was defiant and disruptive," Jimmy said. "I would argue with teachers about everything and pick verbal fights with other kids. Verbal only, never physical. Never."

In the eyes of psychiatrists, Jimmy manifested most, but not all, of the symptoms of Oppositional Defiant Disorder, a condition in which a child displays argumentative behavior toward people in authority.

"Oppositional defiant disorder (ODD) includes a frequent and ongoing pattern of anger, irritability, arguing and defiance toward parents and other authority figures. ODD also includes being spiteful and seeking revenge," the Mayo Clinic notes on its website. "These emotional and behavioral issues cause serious problems with family life, social activities, school, and work."

Jimmy's grandparents didn't know what the scientists and psychologists called it, but they knew something was wrong with the child. "Soon after attending early middle school, school officials informed me and my husband that [Jimmy] needed special attention care, which resulted in his placement into special education programs," Polina recalled. "[Jimmy's] comprehensive level was severely low, he was unable to mentally concentrate on any one subject for a very long time and was subsequently diagnosed as having chronic Attention Deficit Disorder, ADD."

His grandfather explained how that experience affected Jimmy.

"Polena and I enrolled him in school, and it was clear that he had self-control issues. [Jimmy] was still having trouble controlling himself in class. He did have some success in school and was awarded a couple of certificates for achievement."

Like all kids with troubled school careers, Jimmy frequently moved from school to school.

"He was placed in another grade school that had a better program to treat students with ADD. Polena and I took him to the Riverside County Health Department Mental Department to be evaluated by a psychiatrist. He continued to struggle through middle school."

Jimmy's loving grandparents took a great deal of interest in his academic career, such as it was.

"Polena and I were at meetings with the school on a regular basis. [Jimmy] was in a program called IEP. At that point, the school would not let him attend classes unless he was under medication. The medication was Ritalin and a long list of other very powerful drugs. [Jimmy] always complained that the drugs were not good for him, but the school would not allow him to attend classes unless he was drugged."

It wasn't all school, drugs, and chores on the ranch. James's mother, (Jimmy's great grandmother) also lived on the site. Jimmy was devoted to her, his grandparents recalled.

"While growing up on our ranch, [Jimmy] was forever noted as being a loving grandson. [He] was eager to please, he never displayed any characteristics of displaying violence, I never knew Patrick wanting to strike another person, he seemed shy of others when first meeting them," Polina remembered.

"[Jimmy] seemed to have a child-like mentality over the years from which he never grew out of. [Jimmy] was afraid of physical pain, and he was forever receptive to my and my husband's instruction. I found him easy to manage as he did what he was told to do around the house and ranch."

None of it mattered. Like his mother had done before him, eventually Patrick James up and left the ranch for the bright lights of Hollywood.

No, it wasn't his idea. It wasn't that he was searching for somewhere where he would fit in and be accepted.

"I was high school age and acting out more than ever," Jimmy would later recall. "I wasn't violent in any way. I was just oppositional, impulsive, and a real problem. My grandparents just couldn't cope with me anymore.

"One day, after school, I went to get on the school bus home, and they wouldn't let me on. Instead, law enforcement picked me up and took me. I was placed in juvenile hall. From there in several group homes. The abuse in some of them was horrific, and I ran away.

"I was in five group homes altogether and ran away from all of them. I even ran as far as Texas, got in trouble there, and was sent back to California. As I was seventeen with a history of running away, no group home wanted me.

"Well, the day I turned eighteen, someone from Riverside Juvenile Hall drove me to the bus station, bought me a ticket, and escorted me on the bus to Hollywood. It wasn't my idea, but I had no choice in the matter.

"When I got off the bus, I just wandered around. I had nowhere to go and nothing to do when I got there. Thankfully, I met Kelley Leigh, and she took me in, fed me, and did her best to educate me about living on the street."

"I was young, naïve, and well, you know what happened; I hooked up with Audrey, she got pregnant, and then we both started spending more time with Mark. And the next thing we knew, we're in a play that was written before we ever showed up. I guess Mark took one look at us and thought we were perfect casting."

"Jimmy was a total sweetheart," said the woman who would become nearly a surrogate mother to him, Kelley Leigh.

"I did my best to warn him of the dangers of street life, but I couldn't be with him twenty-four/seven, plus he was like any other boy his age physically. In other words, he had a great deal of sexual energy. He needed a girlfriend."

FIRST LOVE

Girls on the street need a sense of security and emotional safety; both are rare commodities.

Audrey found her sense of security with Jimmy, the childlike, honest, eager to please Patrick James Kitlas, whom she met in June 2004. He was the father of her unborn child.

She liked him because he was kind, treated her with gentle consideration, never hit her nor anyone else—an admirable quality not always found among immature men in street relationships.

"Audrey was very protective of him," Kelley recalled. "She made sure he was never alone too long. She was a big influence in his life, and he really tried to make her happy."

"I met her at a drop-in center," Jimmy recalled. "She seemed a shy Polynesian girl."

At five foot three, Audrey was shorter than Jimmy. Jimmy saw her as well-built and healthy. Her hair was brown, long, and straight. She mostly wore it in a ponytail, but sometimes she just let it hang down loose.

She tended to wear clothes that flattered her.

"Her overall appearance was that of a beautiful woman who I was madly in love with then. Her appearance was smiling. Laughing. Playful. Clean no matter what," Jimmy said.

"She has brown eyes that shine funny, but in a good way when the sun hits 'em in the morning," Jimmy recalled.

She was playful and quick to laugh. He was also struck by her quirky looks.

"She was all dimples when she smiled. The left one was deeper than the right one. And her teeth were so beautiful and white. They showed through."

Audrey's skin was tan and smooth and she had a tattoo on her left arm, but after 20 years, Jimmy can't remember what it was.

He does remember that "when she giggled it sounded like the rain. She would playfully sing my name. She would always know my moods and be very touchy when people talked about me when I wasn't around.

"I later met her parents and her grandparents. They all seemed to get along fine. I guess she left home just to have more personal freedom, self-exploration, maybe sexuality. She was very open sexually. She thought I was the father of her child."

Expecting the arrival of their little homeless bundle of joy, the couple utilized whatever services for homeless youth existed in Hollywood. More often, they relied upon the kindness of strangers.

More and more, they kept running into Mark Itaev.

Finally, Audrey was introduced to Mark by Mark's girlfriend. At the time, Mark was married and in his 30s. The girlfriend was 17.

After connecting with Mark, the group mainly hung out and devised ways to scam.

"He was this big Russian guy, and I could tell right away that when he walked into a room a lot of people respected him. He brought a lot of gravitas into a room," Jimmy said. "Mark seemed to be this Russian guy who was well-respected among other Russians.

"I figured that if I worked hard enough and impressed this guy that I wouldn't just be this teenager hanging out on the corner. I'd be able to make my own way, make my own life. You know? That was my teenaged thinking."

As Jimmy recalls, Mark picked up on his insecurities and played them to manipulate the younger man.

"So, he started buying me clothes, buying me food, and we'd go pick up money from people. He always had money.

"The first time he ever had me do anything illegal was he had me carry his gun. That way, if we were ever caught, he would be let free and I would take the blame for it. He said that way, he would be protected."

The gun, a modified 9mm Beretta with an extended muzzle, was fitted with a flash suppressor. There was always one round in the chamber and a full clip. Mark carried it everywhere he went.

Mark, whose face bore slight acne scars, had big wide shoulders. "Big, big hands," Jimmy recalled. "He was a very physically imposing person. Short brown hair, stubble on his face."

It seemed to Jimmy like Mark was always frowning.

He was "really intimidating."

A side benefit of Jimmy and Audrey's friendship with an older and more confident street person was that Mark's experience at grifting ensured they had food, cash, and a place to crash every night for a few weeks. They began to rely on him.

Jimmy said some girls at the shelter taught him some basic Russian. He found that he had a knack for languages. And as he began learning how to speak Russian, it gave him a sense of accomplishment.

"When I first met Mark," Jimmy said, "I thought he was a very kind person who was interested in my life and wellbeing, and that he cared about my girlfriend too. He would get us a place to sleep, and he bought us some meals that we really enjoyed. At some point, Mark began making suggestions to me and Audrey where he said that Audrey and I could make a lot of money if we did exactly what he told us to do. He wanted us to take checks and cash them and bring the money back.

"During our interactions, he would sometimes threaten me that if I ever told anyone about what he was doing, I would be severely dealt with from the Russian Mafia. The same threat applied to Audrey."

Mark could be intimidating, and he often bragged about how he was a *druzia* (a friend) and was hooked up with the *Bratva* (the Russian Mafia).

He explained to Jimmy the difference between the various classes of the Russian criminal underworld.

"And I can never be *padruzhai* because I'm not Russian, right? I'm not from, like, anywhere over there. I have no Russian blood at all," Jimmy said.

"The guys that are actually from Russia are called *druzia*. They are like the Old World mobsters. They're mostly, like, former military."

If they would come around, getting an org chart or figuring out who was who was "not something you asked," Jimmy said. "I just tried to make myself as likeable as possible."

Although Mark operated via intimidation, that wasn't really Jimmy's way. He preferred to remain in the shadows, soaking up what he could.

"The only time I really went off by myself was when he told me to go deliver something like an envelope or whatever, and it was really just pretty much always around West Hollywood, in the region between La Brea and Doheny.

"Basically, we were, like, scamming people's IDs. That was his thing. I didn't understand how it worked, but I remembered how he would do it. People would bring him mail and he would take checks and put some kind of liquid on them and the writing would come off.

"Then, he would write in his own amount and then he could deposit that into a checking or a bank account that he opened in my name, and then he would have me pull that money out."

Jimmy would hand over whatever he got from his account to Mark. He wasn't cut in. By his reckoning, he was impressing Mark and the higher-ups by being a good worker.

"Occasionally, there would be, like, side benefits. Like everyone once in a while, he gave me a hotel room, and whenever we were together, he would buy me, like, food and drinks and tobacco. But there was no real tangible benefit. That was, like, a fringe benefit of just being around him because if he's hungry, he's going to eat, which meant I'd eat too."

Jimmy imagined he was living a life in the underworld like those he had seen in any number of Hollywood biopics.

"I envisioned myself, like, in the movies, like, and that was my mentality. At the time, I was, 'Oh. Okay. It's just like in the movies. I'm going to be, like, a made guy. I'll have this nice house, a nice car. I'll be safe, and I can just quit. I can just walk away and keep everything that, that I earn doing these things.'"

One thing the older man failed to mention to either Jimmy or Audrey was that he had another job: he was a confidential informant for the FBI.

As such, Mark routinely helped law enforcement gain insight into local drug smugglers, bank robbers, and assorted other criminals. In return, they sometimes turned a blind eye to his activities.

Court records show that in the spring and early summer of 2004, Mark ran an identity theft scam that gave him access to government issued IDs, bank accounts, and high-limit credit cards in other people's names.

FELONIES

California's attorneys general, both past and present, are exceptionally proactive in fighting and prosecuting identity theft.

Felonies aren't free. You do the crime, you pay with universal currency: time—the one thing everyone has, although no one knows how much.

There is an adage asserting that a man who lies is a man who will steal. After all, once you have stolen the truth, you will steal anything. An equally known adage says, "The truth will out." In other words, you can steal the truth, conceal the truth, but the truth shall be released and revealed.

There is a more recent adage that honestly states, "It all comes out in the wash. It is just the spin cycle that makes you crazy."

When Mark, who had a gambling addiction and spent hours in various casinos, put his spin on it, the truth could be crazy-making.

In the case of Douglas Wayne Kevorkian, whose ID turned up in Mark's hands one night at a poker table, it was a masterclass in crazy-making at the worst place to be a con man—a California casino.

WHAT ARE THE ODDS?

Casinos—especially low-rent California card rooms—haven't only seen it all; they anticipate it. There isn't any form of fraud that they haven't seen before, and they recognize it immediately.

Located in a gritty neighborhood just east of downtown L.A., the Commerce Casino sits in the heart of L.A. County's corruption corridor.

Essentially a stretch of the 710 Freeway that runs north from the port of Long Beach along the Los Angeles River toward the rail yards in Vernon, the Corruption Corridor is lined by several small industrial suburbs like Bell Gardens, Cudahy, Mayflower, Huntington Park, and South Gate. A lot of the money that flows into those cities flows through Commerce.

There is a saying around L.A. that if the suburb where you live has Gardens or Park in the name, it is probably neither.

Cities in the Corruption Corridor are known for their less-than-savory government, their high rates of un-reported crime, unmanageable traffic, and pollution.

Much of the local power structure is embedded in fat cat political positions like water boards and joint powers authorities, which govern from behind the scenes by bid rigging, bribery, and extortion.

The Commerce Casino is a palace amid the squalid sprawl. Inside, it is brightly lit. Girls in short skirts and tights service the winners, while the losers, many with poor dental hygiene and holes in their shoes, wander around the main floor looking for dropped chips and praying they don't get tossed by security.

Too many of these men find shelter in their cars at night before returning to menial day jobs where they can get enough coins together on a paycheck to go back to the casino and blow it.

Elsewhere in the casino, there are rooms where the Everyman can go to play cards and high-roller rooms that offer Chinese dominoes and Pai Gow to Asian residents of the region and tourists from around the world.

A twenty-four/seven operation, the casino is a good place to either have fun or the worst night of your life. It really depends on who you are and what you're made of.

The thing about an operation like Commerce is that the owners and pit bosses aren't easily fooled.

Mark Itaev should have known better than to try a scam there. On April 24, 2004, he walked in with a fake ID and credit card, both in the name of Douglas Wayne Kevorkian. Security, trained to spot fraud, caught it instantly.

"I never gave Itaev permission to use my name," Kevorkian later said.

Deputies were called. Mark, still claiming to be Kevorkian, admitted to the fake ID, saying, "It'd take too long to get a real one."

Arrested and booked at the East L.A. jail, he was out the next morning, the case mysteriously dropped.

A month later, Mark's schemes caught up with him again, this time at a Manhattan Beach hotel on May 27, 2004.

It began when Jimmy, who was high on speed, had a run-in with the police in Manhattan Beach, a bedroom community on the ocean about 20 miles west of Commerce, across the vast expanse of Central Los Angeles between the L.A. River and the Pacific Ocean.

"I remember going into Blockbuster to buy batteries," he said. "The clerk called the police and told them I had a gun in my waistband. I didn't."

Within minutes, police arrived at the scene, ready to handle the call. They encountered Jimmy later. He was unarmed.

Like a bad episode of the popular television show *Cops*, "They surrounded me and took me down," he recalled. "They kept screaming, 'Where's the gun?'"

Once the situation was under control, Jimmy explained he didn't have a gun. When asked, he said he was staying at a local hotel. The officers wanted proof and took him there.

When the investigating officers arrived at the Residence Inn on Sepulveda Boulevard, they knocked on the door of the room where Jimmy and Audrey were staying. Mark answered the door. When asked for identification, Mark said his name was Douglas Kevorkian. He reached behind a wall panel near the room's air conditioner and produced an ID.

Audrey was also there.

The two cops asked to look inside the room and when Mark gave the okay, the officers found two handgun-shaped lighters. Court documents said, "Officers also found a number of documents throughout the suite: bank documents, account statements, passwords, PIN numbers, practice signatures, identification cards, driver's licenses, and credit cards. They found checks with [Jimmy's] name on them, but no false identification in his name."

As they were about to search more, their police radios crackled to life. There was a robbery in progress down the street. The beat cops left the scene in a hurry to respond to the robbery call.

The next morning, two detectives returned to the Residence Inn and knocked on Mark's door. Audrey answered. Again, Mark identified himself as Douglas Kevorkian. And again, the police entered the room.

"Mark had this illegal shit all over the room," Jimmy said. "All his crime stuff was there."

The cops found various documents and acid for washing signatures away, and Mark was arrested. It was stuff Mark carried around in the trunk of his car along with drugs, guns, fake IDs, and stolen mail.[2]

Mark Itaev had been teaching Jimmy the tools of his trade: drug dealing, ID theft, and check washing.

"I don't know where he got the equipment from. To the police it was super suspicious. They took a bunch of photographs and bagged everything up. Then they took Mark to jail and left Audrey and me behind."

Mark was released within 24 hours. Jimmy thought it was weird.

"During this entire time period, Lane and Kitlas were becoming more and more dependent upon Mark Itaev's so-called generosity," recalled Kelley. "Neither of them had any personal interest in becoming part of his identity theft scams. Audrey was adamant that the only reason Shadow was going along with any of it was because Itaev pressured the kid, mocking and threatening him. You must remember that he was like a little kid. He had no guile, no impure motives, and only wanted to protect Audrey and be accepted."

Soon afterward, the trio took up residence at a Travelodge in nearby El Segundo.

Audrey said it was there she heard Mark explain to Jimmy how to fill out bank loan documents in his name, using his true social security number.

"He would drive us around to various banks," said Audrey, "and have Shadow fill out or submit those documents."

---

2. Request for Certificate of Appealability Pursuant to Fed. R. App. P. 22 & 28 U.S.C. § 2253(c), *Kitlas v. Haws*, No. 2:08-cv-06651-GHK (LAL) (C.D. Cal. 2016).

On June 2, the cops came to the door of the room they shared.

Again, Mark was arrested.

When he was booked, he identified himself as Douglas Kevorkian.

Jimmy and Audrey were let go. They headed back to West Hollywood.

When Mark was released two days later, he caught up with Jimmy and Audrey at the C & C Internet Café and said he had a great idea about taking over the lease at an apartment on Sierra Bonita.

Mark didn't say who currently lived in that apartment, but it is a name Jimmy would remember for years afterward: Aleksandr Markzitser.

WAR AND PEACE

To Jimmy, Mark was a cinematic role model. He was like a character in a mob movie. He was connected and earning. In the context of the Russian mob, or *Bratva,* Russian for brotherhood, "earning" refers to generating criminal profits, a portion of which must be contributed up the chain of command. This concept is central to the criminal hierarchy, particularly for the elite known as *vory v zakone,* or "thieves-in-law."[3]

Jimmy hoped that by being pliable and hardworking, the men in Mark's clique of mobsters would accept him.

If so, he would be in a brotherhood, a family that gave him the equivalent of unconditional something—maybe not love, but something. Jimmy knew Mark was part of a family, a brotherhood.

Jimmy didn't know Mark's uncle Meir Itaev, also known as Mike Itaev, but Uncle Meir was, by 2004, already a well-known name to the FBI, the DEA, and other federal agencies concerned with activities of the Russian mob in the United States.

Despite his established reputation as a man allegedly involved in a variety of criminal endeavors, Meir "Mike" Itaev is also known as an exceptionally kind, generous,

---

3. https://www.ojp.gov/ncjrs/virtual-library/abstracts/thieves-professing-code-traditional-role-vory-v-zakone-russias

compassionate man with a soft spot in his heart for disadvantaged kids.

Meir came from Russia with the wave of Russian immigrants in 1977 and settled briefly in Brooklyn's Brighton Beach neighborhood.

By the early 1980s, he was living in L.A. and doing what he could to buy and manage a restaurant.

Eventually, that dream came true. In 1986, Itaev, a self-described chef and restaurant administrator, partnered with Michael Kishner and Vincent Giuliana to buy Vickman's Restaurant at 8th and Merchant, east of downtown on the edge of the produce district but still across the river from East L.A. It was close enough to town that judges, city officials, cops, and even some celebrities were regulars for breakfast and lunch inside the modest, white brick building that featured communal tables—like the more famous Philippe, across from Union Station on Alameda.

The thing about Vickman's that made it especially popular was that it opened at 3:00 a.m., just after the bars closed and just before work in the nearby L.A. Produce Market began. Customers lined up daily for a seat and a memorable meal.

The partners, including Itaev, paid $1.2 million for the deli and bakery that had catered to Angelenos since opening in 1919 at First and Spring in downtown. The Vickman family hoped that Itaev and his partners would treat the business with the same reverence they had treated it for years.

"We wanted people who were young, experienced, and had their own money in it," Harry Vickman said.

The honeymoon didn't last long. In June 1993, Vickman's closed its doors for good. According to *The L.A. Times*, owner Ilya Kleinman stopped paying the Vickmans rent money on the building.

Standing in front of a glass case loaded with cakes and pies, Kleinman, a Russian immigrant, explained to a reporter that his Russian business partners had skipped out. Running a mostly empty 15,000-square-foot restaurant in a neighborhood that was quickly slipping into disrepair wasn't something that he could sustain.

The next time Itaev appeared in *The L.A. Times*, Meir Itaev was under arrest for participating in a novel variation on the most lucrative and least dangerous enterprise of organized crime: gasoline tax evasion.

A federal government task force estimated that the U.S. lost between $5 and $10 billion in the 1970s and 1980s because of gasoline tax evasion. And even though the feds cracked down during the Reagan years, the Italian and Russian mobs working together in New York found loophole after loophole that made gas tax scams work.

Michael Franzese, a caporegime in the Colombo crime family operating in Brooklyn, recalled that in the 1980s, Russian mobsters in Brighton Beach were pulling down millions with a single gas tax scam. Soon, the Russians and Italians were working together.

"The scam was so simple, it's hard to believe no one thought of it before," said Franzese, who is shown as a character in the film *Goodfellas*.

Essentially, the scammer sets up a gas station and collects taxes from customers, but they pay none to the state or the feds and instead pockets the dough. Franzese claims that at the height of his career as a gas tax scammer, he was raking in $8-12 million a week.

The gas tax fraud "was the biggest scam, or business on the street," he added.

"I had one of the biggest things the mob had ever seen before," Franzese has said. "I want to address my relationship with the mobsters from Russia. The Russian mob are great guys, some of the best partners I ever had. Stand up guys, at least with me they were, we did some great business together."

The way it came together, from Franzese's perspective, was organic. Every Monday night, he entertained ideas on money-making schemes from the neighborhood.

"You know, a lot of people think that we mob guys sit around at our social clubs and we devise these elaborate scams," he said. "To infiltrate a business doesn't always happen that way. It's manufactured most of the time. We have people from a certain business that come to us, want to defraud their company, want to make a few extra bucks. They come to us for protection, they come to us for help to implement that scheme, whatever they had—obviously for money if they needed it. That happens quite a bit, certainly happened quite a bit with me, as a matter of fact.

"I had a special place every Monday night... anybody that wanted to present [an idea] could come on Monday and offer a business offer to me. I had lines out the door with people coming that had different ideas, so on and so forth. Some of them were good, most of them I passed on, but that's how many business opportunities that came my way because of who I was."

It was during one of those sessions that Franzese was approached by Lawrence Salvatore Iorizzo, a wiseguy who was skimming off gas taxes but needed a larger organization—like the Columbo family—backing him.

In the 1980s, New York's gasoline wholesale tax laws were riddled with loopholes. Multiple wholesalers could own large volumes of fuel, but only one—the "burn" company—had to pay the taxes. The mob simply set up dummy corporations and a fall guy to take the blame, much like the schemes in *Goodfellas*, where Franzese was portrayed as "Monkey Man."

For example, a Polish immigrant housepainter who spoke no English was listed as president of Shoppers Market Wholesale Inc., the tax-liable entity, per a 1986 *New York Times* report.

After Lawrence Iorizzo explained the scheme to Michael Franzese, they scaled it up for massive profits, despite its simplicity.

Today, Franzese is a motivational speaker sharing his redemption story through events, books, and Christian ministry; he also runs Franzese Wine, applying mob lessons to business.[4]

"The Russians had that idea also, but we were able to implement it better and bigger than anyone else and that's because, you know, I was able to make contacts, keep other people out, and really put a plan and mechanism together that allowed us to defraud the government for several years without getting caught," Franzese said. "It was a very elaborate scheme."

Early on, when the Columbo family began taking over gas stations, they ran into a group of Eastern European mobsters running a similar tax fraud play out of Brighton Beach, a traditionally Jewish enclave on the southern edge of Brooklyn.

What they didn't know was this group of Russians was under the protection of the Lucchese crime family and specifically caporegime Anthony "Gaspipe" Casso, a notorious mob killer feared for his ruthless adherence to the code of La Cosa Nostra.

Like Franzese, Casso allowed the Brooklyn Russians to make money in the gas tax business, provided they kicked up profits to him. The Russians respected Gaspipe and he respected them—even though the Russian and Italian mobs are very different.

The Italians quickly learned what federal agents had suspected about the Russians. They had a "remarkable

---

4. The narrative draws from Michael Franzese's account of the scam with Lawrence Iorizzo; the Shoppers Market case from "Brooklynite Pleads Guilty to Evading State Gas Tax," *The New York Times*, Aug. 30, 1986. (Reporting Polish-born house painter as president of Shoppers Marketing Inc., the "burn" company liable for taxes).

aptitude for sophisticated white-collar crime. They are ruthless, employing threats, intimidation, and violence to further their aims. They are very adaptable. They are not monopolistic. They are very fluid," said Edward L. Federico Jr., former Director of National Operations for Criminal Investigations at the Internal Revenue Service.

According to Federico, in the 1980s, gasoline taxes accounted for about 70 percent of the $20 billion in motor fuel taxes collected every year by the feds in the mid-1990s.

"To give you an idea of the money involved, an average tanker truck holds 8,000 gallons of gasoline. The combined federal and state taxes per gallon can exceed 40 cents, so the average tax per tanker is $3,200. The complicated 'daisy chain' schemes devised by the Russians puts that $3,200 per tanker into their pockets instead of into the pockets of the United States Treasury," Federico said.

What started out as a novel fraud scheme contrived on Long Island quickly evolved into a billion-dollar-a-year business, and everybody in the Russian and Italian mobs were getting rich.

The idea that fueled dreams in Brighton Beach was making things brighter in Los Angeles, but there were other things imported from the East Coast as well—not all of them positive, many of them violent, and at least one that would drastically impact the career of Meir Itaev.

THE RUSSIANS ARE COMING

In the 1970s, Russians such as Meir Itaev gravitated upon arrival in the U.S.A. to Brighton Beach because it felt safe.

They were among their own people and in that environment, the mobsters knew that chances of getting ratted out were slim.

"Almost any case involving Russians is somehow linked to Brighton Beach," NYPD Detective Dan Mackey of the 60th Precinct told *The New York Times.* "It's the first spot they go to when they arrive in the country."

The Q Line subway, which originates in the Upper East Side in Manhattan, runs on an elevated track in Brighton Beach over Brighton Beach Boulevard. The scene is as picturesque as you might imagine and just like any movie you've seen of the area.

The street is lined with delis, jewelers, furriers, cultural clubs, and grocery stores. It isn't too uncommon on the street to see a group of men gathered, smoking cigarettes, drinking strong coffee, and speaking to one another in Russian.

One of the early leaders of the Russian gangsters in New York was the very dapper Evsei Agron, who was known to extort money from fellow immigrants through his expert use of a cattle prod.

Agron was a known *vor v zakone*, a top class of gangster with deep roots in the Russian prison system. *Vor* ran the black market in the Soviet Union and Eastern Europe.

Although he surrounded himself with bodyguards, Agron got shot in the neck in January 1984. When detectives came around asking questions, he told NYPD that he would take care of the attacker on his own. It wasn't the first time he told the cops that. It would be the last.

A year later, on May 4, 1985, Agron was shot again. This time it was fatal. Moments before the slaying, Agron's men had mysteriously disappeared from outside his apartment.

The first godfather of the U.S. Russian Mafia, Agron was listed as vice president of a fitness club that was tied to the Colombo family and Michael Franzese's father John (Sonny) Franzese.

But it wasn't the Italians behind the hit. Agron was killed because he pushed for his own cut of the growing gas tax scam. The name of his killer remains unknown to this day.

Within a few hours of Agron's killing, his bodyguard, Boris "Biba" Nayfeld, was working for a new boss: Marat Yakovlevich Balagula.

An immigrant math genius who had moved to New York from the Soviet Union with his wife and children in 1977, Balagula was part of a second wave of 300,000 mostly Jewish immigrants set free by the USSR as part of a larger agreement with the U.S.

Upon arrival, Balagula told immigration officials he came to the United States to escape anti-Semitism in Russia and to raise his children in a free society, even though he had never been inside a temple, didn't know the Torah or keep the Sabbath.

It made for good Cold War theater. Customs bought the story of a family man fleeing godless communism for First Amendment rights. Within hours, Balagula was operating free and clear in New York City.

The feds were slow to react to the growing threat, and the NYPD not only had few officers who spoke Russian; it had even fewer officers who were willing to tackle the complex problem.

Upon arrival in New York, Balagula and his family first settled in Washington Heights and for a while, Balagula labored in a factory, cutting textiles.

It was there he met Evsei Agron and became the mobster's accountant and confidant. By 1980, he was earning enough money to buy the Odessa Restaurant and nightclub on Brighton Beach Avenue in Brooklyn.

The spot quickly became filled with leggy, blonde Russian prostitutes hoping to score. It was the place where the Russian mafiosos made their deals.

Bodyguard Boris Nayfeld was part of that wave seeking a better life, and as *The Times of Israel* reported in 2018, he turned to crime as soon as he arrived in New York.

The bald-headed and imposing Nayfeld was unashamed of his lifestyle, often sitting for interviews and talking in detail about the hits, the scams, and the sex that came with the gangster lifestyle.

While there were legitimate victims of persecution among the group, the USSR used the opportunity presented by asylum in the United States to set free some of its most dangerous criminals—a tactic Cuba would repeat later in the decade.

In remarks to a U.S. Senate Panel titled "Russian Organized Crime in the United States," Senator William Roth, a Montana Republican, likened the Russians to Bonnie and Clyde gone international. His remarks to the panel were squarely pointed at Balagula.

"Russian organized crime presents a textbook example of what I have referred to as the new international criminals; they are a breed set apart from traditional organized crime. Despite having roots that can be traced back to earlier times, criminals from the former Soviet Union have thrived by adapting to and exploiting modern technology.

"They have created global communication networks using satellite telephones, cellular clone phones, and encrypted fax machines. Combined with relaxed travel restrictions and a greatly increased volume of international trade, these developments have allowed criminal organizations based in one country to extend their operations throughout the world.

"Russian organized crime, in particular, conducts complex fraud schemes, traffics in narcotics, practices extortion, and even commits murder without regard to international borders," the senator remarked.

Or, as one expert put it, American mobsters play checkers, the Russian gangsters play chess.

Of all the Russians pulling scams in Brooklyn, it was Balagula whom Anthony "Gaspipe" Casso of the Lucchese family wanted to partner with. Gaspipe had a good relationship with Balagula.

Balagula had Casso's protection. When a fellow Russian threatened to kill him because he wasn't sharing his windfall, it caused Balagula to have a heart attack.

When he explained to Casso what happened, Casso set up a meeting with the would-be killer and promised to pay him on Balagula's behalf.

When the Russian thug who had been threatening Balagula showed up for a sit-down, he was killed on the spot by two of Casso's men. It sent a strong message to the neighborhood, and to the Russians and Italians that Balagula was connected to the Five Families and that he should be left alone.

Michael Franzese didn't get the memo right away.

When Columbo muscle went to shake Balagula down, it was Gaspipe who stepped in, this time working out an arrangement that allowed Franzese to own stations on Long Island and reap his rewards there.

Years later, Franzese would brag about it as a win for himself and the Colombo family.

The attempted shakedown of Balagula by the Colombo crew resulted in a sit-down at Brooklyn's 19th Hole Social Club, a Lucchese hang-out in Bensonhurst at 86th Street and 14th Avenue.

After the sit-down, Franzese said, "We were able to get along," explaining he offered a 25-percent cut from his gas stations to the Russians. Balagula hesitated at first but ultimately said yes.

"That's how we got together and from that point on, I want to tell you we earned hundreds of millions of dollars together... The Russians made money; my guys made money. Everybody was doing it," he continued.

"I let the Russians have their turn. They made plenty of money. To me, these guys were very, very loyal, they were very smart what I loved about them, they were not afraid of the criminal justice system here. One of them... had did some time in a Russian prison. He said, 'Michael, the prisons in America are walking the park.'

"Like I said, they were very smart, and I enjoyed that. They were probably some of the best partners I ever had."

For Balagula, there were other benefits to partnering with the Italians. For example, Casso had two NYPD detectives and at least one FBI agent on his payroll.

The detectives, Louis Eppolito and Stephen Caracappa, would later be implicated in several murders, including a mistaken identity killing. Both were sentenced to a New York state prison.

When you're defrauding the U.S. government out of hundreds of millions of dollars in tax money, it is easy to understand how those assets can be acquired. Money talks. Bullshit walks. Casso only cared about money, and the Russians knew how to keep him happy.

It was only a matter of time before the details of the lucrative gas tax scam made their way from New York to Southern California, where Russians, who had moved west from New York, were setting up shop.

When it went national, Congress sat up and took notice.

During a 1996 election year appearance before the U.S. Senate's Committee on Governmental Affairs, the Russian mob got a full hearing.

According to Senator William Roth of Delaware, a whole host of bad guys from foreign countries were doing bad things in America. The Russians were hooking up with Asian gangs to bring heroin to the U.S.; with Columbian gangs to bring South American cocaine to Europe; and these mobsters commanded an army of anonymous Russian hitmen who could appear in the U.S., strike a target, then vanish without a trace.

On May 15, 1996, lawmakers, including Roth, gathered in a hearing room at the Dirksen Senate Office Building in the nation's capital to discuss organized crime. This time, Italian mafiosos like Joe Valachi or leaders of the La Cosa Nostra weren't under the magnifying glass.

And it wasn't like the Senate hearing scene in *The Godfather*, where Frank Pentangeli testifies about Michael Corleone's criminal activities. Instead, former capos and underbosses of the Russian mob were taking the heat.

After Roth made his remarks, FBI Director Louis Freeh said, "The Russian Mafia is the most lethal, deadliest, and feared criminal organization in the world. According to the CIA, they are a bigger threat to our national security than ISIS or Al Qaeda."

As Freeh told it, following the collapse of the Soviet Union in 1991, organized criminals began to take over Russia's economy and spawned thousands of powerful crime gangs, some of which established émigré communities in the United States.

INSIDE THE RUSSIAN MOB

This link between crime and Russia's economy is accurate and correct, according to Stan Nechayev, a career criminal in the Russian mob (retired).

"Yeah, it's the same machine," Nechayev said.. "It's so glued together with the government that it's almost inseparable. Corruption is a big thing in my country, and it always has been; therefore, it's all linked together, it's a proven fact, since the first day. It used to be much worse," he explained.

"I know they compare 1930s Chicago to Russia. But Chicago is a newborn baby compared to the Soviet Union when everything fell apart. It was just insane."

According to American government commentators, becoming a career criminal in Russia is a well-established career choice, right up there with firefighter, dentist, or sex worker.

"It is an accepted and normal part of our lives," Stan acknowledged. "I didn't know any better. That was the cool thing to do. It starts at an early age. At school you want to be cool. Mothers and fathers aren't present. Everybody is working for a few dollars. And this is usually what happens. You go at eight years old and rob your first store. Then you continue doing little stuff, a lot of fighting going on. Then you climb up with time. The older you get, the more sophisticated you become. Basically, you learn new skills."

The FBI emphasizing how ruthless the Russians are compared to other criminal organizations is a generalization decried as such by Stan, among others with true insider knowledge.

"My opinion, you can't put everyone under the same umbrella. You got the Georgian people and they're known for one thing. Then you got Azerbaijanians... and Chechens... some organizations are known for one thing; some are known for something else. It is nothing like the Sicilian or Italian Mafia. Entirely different structure. They have the capos and the bosses, and they answer for everything. Russians are different, they have different groups. They don't have the same boss. If the different groups have a disagreement, there are not gang wars like in Chicago 1930s. Yes, some do murder for hire... those may have a big body count, but the ones making the most money do non-violent white-collar crime. I can't say nobody ever gets hurt, but very few. The different Russian groups have different specialties: some people smuggle drugs, other smuggle chocolate, or cars, or tobacco."

As for former FBI Director Louis Freeh saying, "The Russian Mafia is the most lethal, deadliest, and feared criminal organization in the world," Stan sighs and shakes his head.

"Well, this is Russia's problem. The FBI and the media always make everything way too big. Like I said when I came to America, it's always, 'The Russians are coming, the KGB are coming.' It's always coming and coming and coming. You watch every movie in Hollywood, and you always make Russians look so bad. The media hype is bullshit. Scaring the American public, that's what it's for."

Stan paused, giving his next statement serious thought.

"It is a constant source of amazement that America, a nation of immigrants, promulgates such fear and disrespect for immigrants."

U.S. officials estimated that 20 organized criminal groups of Russian origin were involved in illicit activities in the U.S., and those groups were concentrated in NYC, L.A., and Miami. Their crimes include money laundering, finance fraud, racketeering, and drug trafficking.

As Stan said, unlike the Italian Mafia with its soldiers, capos, and consiglieres, Russian mobsters were generally viewed by federal investigators with boots on the ground as disorganized and unstructured, with no hierarchy or specific chain of command.

On the East Coast, agents saw cases that involved fraud, money laundering, and healthcare scams.

On the West Coast, Russian mobsters were involved in money laundering, check kiting, tax fraud, drug dealing, and extortion.

The one thing that tied them all together though was the gas tax scam.

During testimony, horrified senators learned that "daisy chain" schemes devised by Russians put truckloads of U.S. dollars into the pockets of the *vor*, instead of going to the U.S. Treasury.

Like all good congressional hearings on organized crime, this one had a chart linking Russia to Brighton Beach and then detailing the various organizations around the U.S. Using the charts, it didn't take rocket science to connect the Brighton Beach gangsters to a group of West Coast Russians in Los Angeles running their own set of businesses.

Smack in the middle of the West Coast mob chart was the name Meir Itaev, identified as head of the Itaev Organization, headquartered in West Hollywood and one of 26 Eurasian organized crime groups operating in the U.S., officials explained.

Meir had something in common with L.A.'s most famous gangster of the 1940s, Meir "Mickey" Cohen: his organization also made its dough in and around Hollywood, even if Meir Itaev was nowhere near as flashy as Cohen, who was once featured in an eight-page spread in the January 16, 1950, issue of *LIFE*.

That being said, if you went looking for Meir Itaev, he was easy to find. He was known to be open, approachable, gregarious, and friendly. Just go to Los Angeles's Plummer Park and ask for Meir. After all, some called him "The Godfather of Plummer Park."

PLUMMER PARK

Plummer Park is a West Hollywood neighborhood gathering spot that has been a community center of sorts for Russian immigrants since the late 1970s and early 1980s.

In January 1997, it was the center of the nation's attention following the murder of Ennis Cosby, son of famous (and now disgraced) comedian/TV star Bill Cosby.

Home from college on winter break, Ennis was driving his dark green Mercedes Benz on the 405 Freeway when he had a blowout.

After pulling to the side of the road, Ennis telephoned his girlfriend, Stephanie Crane, who came to rescue him. When she arrived, a man tapped on her window with a gun and demanded she open the car window, or he would kill her.

As Crane pulled away, she heard gunshots and saw the man run away. By the time Crane was able turn her car around and return to the scene, Ennis was dead.

The case immediately turned into a media circus. Leading the way was Harvey Levin, who was reporting anything and everything that he could remotely link to the crime. Most of it was speculative and the rest was straight interference with the investigation.

On top of that, when California Lt. Gov. Gray Davis offered a $50,000 reward for information leading to the arrest and conviction of Ennis's murderer, Republican politicians called foul and demanded to know why Davis would pay rewards for the murder of a celebrity's child, but never offer a similar bounty for murderers in less high-profile cases.

One of those accusing Davis was Assemblyman Gary Miller, who went absolutely ballistic when the reward was offered that wouldn't go for a case that was equally deserving.

Miller would go on to become a U.S. Congressman, and Davis would become California's governor. Both owed their advancement in some part to taking public stances on the Cosby case.

A lot more happened around the Cosby case that called attention to L.A.'s Russian connections and the scabby TMZ-style media that dominated late '90s reporting in the post-O.J. Simpson era.

In a nutshell, the politics of race, class, media ethics, and L.A. gangs all came to the fore and mixed in a pungent stew of lies, half-truths, gossip, and sex.

By the logic of the newly emerging infotainment media, Cosby had to have been murdered for a reason: drugs, a hit, or something involving his dad. We know now that there was a lot of unpleasantness involving Bill Cosby.

Eventually, police narrowed in on a lone suspect in the slaying: Mikhail Markhasev, a drug addict and former honor student, who came to the United States from Ukraine as a toddler with his mother. He got caught thanks to a $100,000 reward offered by the *National Enquirer.*

Even though he never lived close to West Hollywood, upon his arrest, Markhasev, 19, brought the attention of the media onto the neighborhood's immigrant community after he was turned in by an informant who cashed in the $100,000 reward.

The vultures descended in droves to get any scrap of news about the killer they could scrape up from the gutter of rumors, paid sources, and whisper campaigns.

A group of residents held a press conference to decry the media's focus on West Hollywood Soviet Jews, who were alleged to have ties to organized crime. The papers called them "Glastnost Gangsters."

Glastnost was the period of openness in the Soviet Union that coincided with the thawing of relations between Russia and the United States. It created an open door for immigration that to reporters and cops fed the growing Russian gang problem in L.A.

The FBI and L.A. County Sheriff's Department did little to dispel the generalizations.

"Is there a Russian Mafia? I think that's been well-documented," Los Angeles County Sheriff's Lt. Robert Cook said. "There is organized crime being perpetrated by immigrants from the former Soviet bloc. How persistent is it? That's hard to say. We know we have a number of crooks that conspire together."[5]

There was a caveat.

"Ninety-nine-point-nine percent of Russian immigrants are not unlike any other immigrants," Cook said. "Clearly, there are some people who come with the group... that tend to taint the rest."

That was all the leverage the Russians gathered at Plummer Park needed to make their case.

"The media should examine its own face," said Boris Gorbis, a Russian American attorney at the rally. "We resent that when the media uses shortcuts, it does not care about the visceral effects it will have. There is not one single ounce of evidence—not one shred—that there is a single organized, planned, coordinated criminal effort on the part of Russian immigrants."

That being said, regardless of motivation, the media had its reasons for narrowing its focus on Plummer Park.

---

5. SPECIAL TO THE TIMES, "'Russian Mafia' Label Denounced," *The Los Angeles Times*, March 21, 1997, https://www.latimes.com/archives/la-xpm-1997-03-21-me-40610-story.html

In the early 1990s, law enforcement linked several L.A. murders to the Russian *Organitzaya*, which used the park as a place to engage in games of chess and to plot.

The execution-style murders of Andrey Kuznetsov and Vladimir Litvinenko in January 1992, for example, over a dispute regarding profits from a fraud ring, represented the Russian organized crime threat to L.A. in ways that the cops were ready to exploit.

Kuznetsov, a good-looking young man, had the world by the balls. He had escaped the Soviet Union and was now living in style as an art expert in Beverly Hills. Not a bad life swap. Litvinenko's life was nearly as charmed—as a young man, he had done time in the treacherous Soviet Gulag.

Litvinenko and Kuznetsov shared an apartment with two other men and after a dispute between the four, shots were fired, and the art dealer and former criminal were killed.

Their killers cut off the dead men's hands and were in the process of pulling bullets out of the mutilated and lifeless bodies when cops arrived, responding to a neighbor's call about shots fired.

The case was shocking enough that for a while, *The Los Angeles Times* included it on a tour map it published of other famous murders like the Tate-La Bianca slayings and that of Elizabeth Short, the Black Dahlia.

Following the Cosby shooting, California Attorney General Daniel Lungren laid out the landscape of Russian crime operations that supported guys like Kuznetsov and Litvinenko in a report that was heavy on law-and-order political theater and light on facts.

Lungren's intro paragraphs betrayed his political sensibilities and made it clear that he had his eye on running for governor.

"With the demise of the Soviet Union, the world witnessed a breathtaking end to the Cold War and welcomed over 276,600,000 citizens of the 15 new republics to democratic government—and free market capitalism.

"Russian organized crime, unfortunately, has thrived in the new economic system, and has moved beyond Russia's borders. Not surprisingly, law enforcement experts in the United States have detected a Russian organized crime presence in several states, including California.

"The most common criminal enterprises undertaken by Russian organized crime groups in California [which includes groups whose members come from all of the former Soviet republics] at this time appear to be fraud schemes, particularly 'fuel tax frauds' designed to divert fuel tax revenue to the pockets of criminals.

"However, more common organized crime opportunities—extortion, loan sharking, drug trafficking, auto theft, prostitution, and other crimes—have attracted increasing interest among Russian organized crime groups."

Just your run-of-the-mill organized crime set-up. Right?

For the first time ever, courtesy of the Lungren report, the public was given a clear synopsis of the now infamous Kuznetsov and Litvinenko slayings.

"Andrey Kuznetsov and an associate, Vladimir Litvinenko, were shot to death in Kuznetsov's rented house in West Hollywood on January 26, 1992. Kuznetsov, a pretty boy who dated Hollywood actresses, was believed to have been the leader of a Los Angeles fraud ring with ties to Russian organized crime in New York and Russia. His widow claimed he introduced her to Russian organized crime leaders and members in Los Angeles and New York."

What Lungren didn't note was that the Russian killings took place just off the Sunset Strip in a pad not too far from Mickey Cohen's former haberdashery and the place where Aleks Markzitser was killed a few years later.

Bottom line: It was a botched hit. Lungren's report sanitized the crime scene.

"Deputies arrested two Russian emigres at the murder scene. Sergei Ivanov was drenched in blood and carrying a handgun. An accomplice, Alexander Nikolaev, was also arrested with Ivanov.

"Found in the house along with the bodies were numerous boxes of electronic equipment, copiers, TV sets, fax machines, and stereo components.

"Authorities said that most of the equipment was stolen or illegally paid for using fraudulent credit cards and check kiting."

The redacted and cleaned-up public version of the arrest neglected to mention that the clumsy killers were former members of the Soviet Army and that the equipment found at the crime scene was the sort that criminals used in check forging scams.

And herein was the truth about the demise of Kuznetsov and Litvinenko: they were caught up in something bigger than themselves and didn't pay off the right people.

Lungren's report also focused on fuel tax fraud and pointed out that the scams that were prevalent in New York a decade earlier had likely made their way to California.

Now, instead of an elaborate daisy chain of ownership to hide the purchasers of untaxed gasoline, the Russian mobsters in California were more creative. These guys stole jet fuel—a form of diesel—or imported cheap, watered-down gas from Mexico and straight bootlegged the stuff throughout L.A.

Lungren also sensed that there would be more than gas tax scams within the *Organitzaya*.

He theorized that the group would soon be working with a rogue's gallery of dangerous criminals including La Cosa Nostra, La Eme, the Colombian cartels, and white-collar insiders, and had the potential to expand well beyond the second or third tier of organized crime.

"Russian organized crime groups specialize in targets of opportunity and take advantage of bureaucratic mazes to build their profit base. They bring with them knowledge and methods to operate complicated fraud schemes, which allow these white-collar criminals to flourish," Lungren reported.

"While public and law enforcement attention is drawn to gangs and street violence, Russian organized crime groups will make inroads into California using these complex criminal schemes requiring extensive investigative efforts."

Most importantly, the Russians were fearless.

"Members of Russian organized crime groups are violent, but violence is usually employed for specific reasons such as eliminating competition and informants or punishing those who abscond with funds. They are much like the LCN and not like street gangs who use indiscriminate violence," Lungren concluded.

"Law enforcement authorities in California have had several confrontations with crime figures from the former Soviet Union. These crime figures are not afraid of American law enforcement or the criminal justice system and pose a potential threat to police officers."

For reporters and Angelenos who bothered to read Lungren's report, they knew that the characterization was nothing new.

In fact, many remembered that afternoon in the early 1990s when they first became aware of something criminal lurking in the shadows of the neighborhood center at West Hollywood's Plummer Park. That something was a definite and deadly rift that would pit Meir Itaev against a very dangerous Monya Elson.

GLASTNOST GANGSTERS

In the early 1980s, Monya Elson mostly flew under the radar of law enforcement. A player in the Brighton Beach mob, he had ties to and rivalries with both Marat Balagula and Boris Nayfeld.

A squat, powerful guy with a hairline that sometimes resembled a shorter version of Stooge Moe Howard's bowl cut, the olive-complexioned Elson was known to be constantly on the make for a deal: drugs, hookers, gambling, loan sharking, tax scams. Name it, and it is likely Elson was involved at some level. Murder was also his thing.

He disappeared from the East Coast for six years after a drug conviction in Israel and upon his return to New York in 1992, the baby-faced godfather tried to muscle his way back into his old rackets, even as he was reaping the lucrative rewards of a heroin smuggling operation that was nothing short of genius.

Known to some as "The Billion Dollar Don," Monya Elson wasn't sharing those profits. That angered his associates. They wanted him dead.

Elson felt he had been cut out of the gasoline tax scams and believed he was due to get paid. Because he saw himself as the "Godfather," he figured he was entitled to a piece. It wasn't going to be that simple.

As they say, more money, more problems. Sure, the Russians were raking in hundreds of millions of dollars with the tax scam, but they were paying out tens of millions in underworld taxes. Protection from the Italians cost money; coercing corrupt government agents to turn a blind eye carried costs too. Elson's demands didn't wear well.

"He was cocky when he came back," said an insider who asked not to be identified. "And he almost got whacked as a result."

The blowback against the return of Elson resulted in a bloody war among rival factions from New York to L.A., fighting over the income from drugs and tax evasion.

"Monya Elson and a group called 'Monya's Brigada' were indicted by a federal grand jury for, among other crimes, three murders and one attempted murder. This violence reportedly resulted from Elson's desire for recognition and stature. Two of the victims were targeted by Elson because he was jealous of their status in the criminal community."

"There have also been numerous extortions of Russian émigrés in the region. Many of these were committed by enforcers, criminals who specialize in extorting Russian-owned businesses in Brighton Beach and elsewhere.

The enforcers work for whomever pays them. Although occasionally, there may be disputes between individuals or groups regarding certain extortion victims, most of the extortion appears to be opportunistic rather than a systematic approach to obtain power or control. Russian violence is not random in the same sense as the drive-by shootings of street gangs."

Somewhat reassuringly, commissioners added that "Russian émigré criminals appear to exercise some care in choosing their victims and avoiding harm to innocent bystanders."

As to the shootings, murders and attempted murders are chronicled in the report.

"...the Russians' reputation for violence exceeds the reality of its use, at least in the United States. As has been true in United States drug markets, a great deal of

Russian émigré violence is attributable to the unregulated competition that exists in their criminal ventures."[6]

Mentions of Elson in the report not only tied him to acts of extortion and violence in New York; they also linked him to an attempted murder in West Hollywood's Plummer Park and, according to contemporary news reports at the time, Meir "Mike" Itaev, known throughout L.A. as "The Godfather of Plummer Park" was thought to be the guy who wanted Monya dead. Law enforcement alleged he was willing to pay for it.

A report by agents of the U.S. Treasury Department contains this description of an attempted murder that got little press at the time, but to investigators it was the missing link in a giant puzzle.[7]

The November 1992 ambush shooting linked New York to L.A., and both U.S. cities to a growing criminal underworld headquartered in Moscow and Odessa.

Tying Monya Elson to the gas tax scam and drug trade gave agents their clearest picture of the sophistication deployed by the Glastnost Gangsters and their first links to the organization's growth in West Hollywood.

The report begins, "In November 1992, Monya Elson was shot and wounded in Plummers Park, in Los Angeles. Based upon source information and other developments it is believed that Meir Itaev set up this attempt on Elson's life... In June 1993, Itaev sent [a hitman] to New York City to kill [a confidential informant].[8]

---

6. Tri-State Joint Soviet-Emigre Organized Crime Project, Russian-Emigre Organized Crime in the Tri-State Area, New Jersey State Commission of Investigation, 1997, https://nj.gov/sci/pdf/russian.pdf.

7. Federal Bureau of Investigation, Russian / Eurasian Criminal Networks Threat Analysis: Sacramento, New York Area Intelligence Unit (n.d.), https://www.scribd.com/document/562252199/Solntsevo-FBI-undated.

8. Federal Bureau of Investigation, Russian / Eurasian Criminal Networks Threat Analysis: Sacramento, New York Area Intelligence Unit (n.d.), https://www.scribd.com/document/562252199/Solntsevo-FBI-undated.

"In March 1993, Itaev was arrested in California for filing false excise tax forms and he believed that [the informant] somehow was responsible for his arrest. [The informant] was shot and wounded by [the hitman] in the shop that he owns in New York City. He pursued [the hitman] into the street and shot him with an unlicensed gun. [The hitman] was arrested, convicted, and is incarcerated in a prison in upstate New York."

The Treasury Department report described Meir Itaev as a member/associate of the "ORGANIZATSIYA" operating in Los Angeles, California.

If there was money to be made, be it from fuel tax fraud or any other golden opportunity, investigators were well assured that somewhere, somehow, Meir/Mike Itaev would be involved.

There is truth found in this 19th-century proverb: "With fire we test our gold, and with gold we test our servants."

Not all gold glitters, but the attraction of black gold is undeniable.

BLACK GOLD

In the first half of the 20th century, the leading oil producer in the U.S. wasn't Oklahoma or Texas; it was California. That fact alone attracted mobsters, scammers, and sketchy outsiders to the fringes of the production and supply chain. .

Beneath the cotton candy skies, under the orange groves, seeping from below the sandy beaches, and bubbling up in the farm fields of the vast Central Valley, oil and natural gas are the ubiquitous by-products of the Golden State.

It is pumped from the ground in Bakersfield and Oildale, refined in Wilmington and Torrance, and delivered to thousands of wholesalers and tens of thousands of retailers from San Francisco to San Diego. It is then pumped again into the millions of California cars commuting hours to work and back home day after day after day.

The economics of this supply chain are stunning. In 2018, State officials estimated that the industry employed just under 150,000 Californians and contributed $26 billion to the state's economy.

California would be nothing other than a pretty coast with good weather if it wasn't for oil. In fact, a century ago, it was the world's leading producer, with 57 refineries cranking out 186 million barrels of oil annually.

Oil paid for everything that defines California, from the freeways to the studios.

Historian Eric Schlosser told *The New York Times*, "Hollywood was born in the decade from around 1911 to 1921, and oil money financed some of the new films."

According to PoweringCalifornia.com, "Thanks to the oil industry, Los Angeles, Orange, and Kern Counties began to thrive and diversify their economies. California's oil and natural gas production was also instrumental in powering the industries that helped the United States and our allies prevail in World Wars I and II."

One of the swankiest and most exclusive clubs in the L.A. area was the Petroleum Club in Long Beach, a retro '60s Don Draper sort of place replete with a circular bar, a swimming pool, and a menu that always offered Grade A prime rib with a Manhattan on the side.

Oildale in Kern County, the birthplace of country music legend Merle Haggard, is practically nothing but oil wells— thus the name. It can also claim some of the wealthiest Californians as residents.

Business association meetings in the Central Valley are a great example of the reach of oil culture into California lifestyle and politics. If the Chamber wants something and the big oil rep on the board doesn't like it, then kiss your great idea goodbye.

California's oil wealth brings with it many opportunities for corruption. Take, for example, land valuation for the purposes of taxes. A county assessor can consider the amount of oil a particular patch might produce into the valuation of a piece of land.

And when you pencil out property taxes, you can see why the State Treasurer might be interested in the value of land based on its production capabilities, rather than its actual production. The difference could mean millions to the State or millions in savings for the oil company.

Further complicating matters is the fact that once oil is pumped out of the land, it no longer counts against the land's value. In some ways, oil property is the opposite of almost every other property in California as it loses value instead of gaining it.

And once a well is pumped dry, theoretically there is little chance of selling the toxic land the process leaves behind.

The money that flows from California oil fields is anything but clean and tends to dirty anyone who gets close—except perhaps the lucky family in *The Beverly Hillbillies*.

Unscrupulous county assessor's agents have known for years that the easiest way to make some Christmas dough is to undervalue oil fields with the consent of the owner and then take a kickback "tip" on a percentage of the tax savings.

It makes sense that new players to the California scene would want a piece of oil money. There was no better way to get it than to step into the middle of the daisy chain of transactions and get lost or get arrested.

Allegedly, Mike Itaev and his crew got in and got caught.

The *San Jose Mercury News* printed a story about the arrests after they were prompted to do so by an IRS official.

As *Mercury News* writer Rodney Foo explained, the scam relied on counterfeit exemption certificates that enabled the scammers to buy large quantities of fuel tax-free from refineries.

Legitimate wholesalers would collect the federal and state taxes and pay them to the government at the end of every month, collecting them from their gas station customers.

One day after the *Mercury News* story, *The L.A. Times* picked up the narrative. Unlike the *Mercury News*, *The L.A. Times* added "context."

LOS ANGELES TIMES, MARCH 4, 1993

Federal agents this week arrested the suspected organizers of a diesel fuel tax fraud ring as part of a crackdown on schemes that authorities estimate deprive the state and U.S. governments of at least $100 million a year in California.

The move, carried out Tuesday and Wednesday and involving 100 agents, was dubbed "Operation Diesel Storm."

"If we can take out the organization these people are associated with, then we will have dealt a severe blow to motor fuel excise tax evasion in Southern and Central California," said Dennis E. Crawford, chief of the tax agency's criminal investigation division in Los Angeles.

Arrested in predawn raids in Hollywood and North Hollywood were four men including Meir "Mike" Itaev. The arrests went down at apartments in Hollywood and North Hollywood, federal agents reported.[9]

According to the lone remaining published report on the case, the four men were taken to the Metropolitan Detention Center in downtown Los Angeles and held on hefty bail.

Authorities laid out a scheme that mirrored the cons that had been played out in New York. This time, though, instead of gasoline, the fuel involved was diesel, and the untaxed sales sparked nearly an all-out price war among gas stations in California's Central Valley that cater to truckers on the road between L.A. and Frisco.

---

9. Times staff writer, "IRS Agents Arrest Four in Fuel Tax Fraud Ring: Schemes: Operators take advantage of exemptions for certain uses, buying diesel gasoline and reselling it at cut rates," *The Los Angeles Times*, March 4, 1993, https://www.latimes.com/archives/la-xpm-1993-03-04-me-365-story.html.

The IRS claimed Itaev's crew sold its tax-free fuel to gas stations along Highway 99 in the San Joaquin Valley and walked away without paying the 20 cents per gallon tax to the feds or the 17 cents per gallon tax to California.

And in a way, that's what led the IRS to Itaev and his cohorts. Other retailers along the well-traveled corridor between Northern and Southern California began to complain about getting undercut on retail sales. Eventually, the IRS had to do something.

Adding a human touch, perhaps, *The L.A. Times*—in an obvious attempt to appear disdainful—set about interviewing neighbors of the men.

One of the men was suspicious because, according to *The Times* article, he never appeared to work, and several young men hung around his apartment all day talking on their cell phones.

In the 1990s, that was a thing.

That was as far as the story went. The case was dismissed six weeks later with no charges filed. Operation Diesel Storm became Operation Diesel Drizzle.

Meir/Mike Itaev got his bail money back and walked out of court a free man. He would stay under the radar for the next half of the decade.

NOT QUITE SKID ROW

"In case you haven't figured it out, being a homeless teenager is dangerous," Kelley Leigh said. "I'm lucky to be alive. The hell really started when I was fifteen. That's when I was kidnapped, held hostage, raped, sodomized, beaten, abused, and blatantly traumatized."

Kelley had a good, loving mom and older siblings, but an event such as that, especially in puberty, has a serious impact.

"I ran away from home, was arrested, incarcerated, rehabilitated, reimagined, rearrested, laughed at, locked up, overlooked, under-estimated—you throw out an adjective of unpleasant inference and I'm sure I've lived it, seen it, had to deal with it, or cooked it and sold it on the streets of Hollywood. There are dangerous people out there, predators and pedophiles and more under-the-radar illegal criminal aliens than an *X Files* marathon, and enough All-American sociopaths to run for office in every state in the union or pontificate from every church pulpit in Los Angeles County."

Homeless youth face significantly higher mortality rates than their housed peers, with studies indicating that the death rate among homeless youth can be 12 to 40 times higher than that of the general youth population.

A systematic review published in *ScienceDirect* (2023) found that suicide is the leading cause of death among homeless youth, surpassing other causes such as drug overdoses, homicides, accidents, or infectious diseases.

This review highlighted that mortality rates due to suicide in this population are particularly elevated, with risk factors including mental health diagnoses, history of abuse, negative coping strategies, and prolonged homelessness.

Data specific to homeless youth aged 15 to 25 in Hollywood is limited, but national trends suggest that suicide accounts for a significant proportion of deaths among homeless youth in urban settings. For example, the Centers for Disease Control and Prevention (CDC) notes that suicide is the second leading cause of death for youth aged 15 to 24 in the general U.S. population, and the heightened vulnerabilities of homeless youth amplify this risk.

According to University of Toronto psychiatrist and researcher Sean A. Kidd, street youth face many dangers and sources of stress in their lives on the street.

"To support themselves," explains Kidd, "they engage in activities such as trying to find work, seeking money from family or friends, panhandling, prostitution, survival sex, drug dealing, and theft."

Despite their best efforts, Kidd noted, large numbers of homeless youth lack shelter and go hungry, living a life that subjects them to endless ridicule and mockery that takes a severe emotional toll.

These negative experiences are associated with other problems such as poor school performance, conflict with teachers, and behavioral problems in the classroom. All of these start the process of stigmatization because the kids are considered different.

"You look at Shadow's history of behavioral issues due to his inability to stay focused," said Kelley, "and you realize that he suffered from the stigma of being different long before he had the added stigma of being homeless—and that's a double dose of social justification for prejudice to the point of demonization and the presumption of criminality."

Because all street kids are assumed to be criminals, they quickly learn that police service and protection doesn't apply to them. They're denied community security and are often the victims of theft and brutality by local law enforcement.

Bring a homeless teenager accused of a felony to court, and he or she is deemed guilty before any presentation of evidence. Their very existence is one of perpetual guilt—an erroneous assumption seldom corrected by the presentation of evidence.

"The facts seldom correct a presumption of guilt by those who are supposed to presume innocence," Kelley said. "Social stigma permeates every aspect of life, both on the streets and in the privacy of middle-class homes in gated communities."

Steve Kimes, a pastor who ministers to a congregation comprised, in whole or in part, of Christians who find themselves homeless, shared this exemplary anecdote:

"Six police officers came to my church, handcuffed and seated ten people in the parking lot and threatened them verbally. Ten more officers came, with their lieutenant, who asked me, 'Are you the pastor? Does your congregation want people like this here?' I pointed at all the people they had handcuffed and said, 'They ARE my congregation.' The lieutenant turned to his officers and said, 'We aren't wanted here, let's go,' and they all released the folks and left. But not before the officer who started it all screamed at my face for 'enabling these criminals.'"

The first study of the actual criminal aspects of being homeless was conducted by Andrea Solarz. "An Examination of Criminal Behavior among the Homeless" was first presented at the Annual Meeting of the American Society of Criminology (San Diego, CA, November 13-17, 1985).

The primary takeaway from her study was that while illegal activity among the homeless would, at first glance, seem distressing, most illegal acts weren't felonies, were nonviolent, and primarily were related to street-level survival because of the inadequacy of help for the poor and displaced.

Illegal sources of income including selling marijuana (then illegal) and other controlled substances (including prescribed medicines), shoplifting for personal needs, stealing items in order to sell them, and leaving restaurants without paying for meals weren't unusual.

Selling pot was the most mentioned source of illegal income. For about 9% of the participants, their main source of income during the past month was illegal. Panhandling, illegal in some jurisdictions, was reported as a source of income during the past six months by around 11% of the participants.

Most illegal acts committed by the homeless came in the categories of "Supplemental Crimes" and "Crimes of Necessity," which Ms. Solarz defined and explained as follows.

The meager income provided by public assistance, or by part-time or sporadic employment, isn't adequate to provide for shelter, food, and personal needs. Thus, some resort to low levels of criminal behavior to provide small amounts of additional income or resources.

Included in this group are those who illegally supplement welfare payments with work income, those who deal in small amounts of drugs or who sell some of their own prescription medicines, and those who occasionally supplement existing resources by shoplifting food or personal use items. Most of the criminal behavior of those in this study likely falls into this category.

For those who are truly homeless or who find themselves temporarily without shelter or any source of income, criminal activity may become an adaptive behavior necessary for survival. For this group, engaging in illegal behavior is directly related to their state of homelessness.

In this study, participants reported breaking into cars to obtain shelter for the night, eating in restaurants and then leaving without paying for their meal, living in abandoned buildings (i.e., trespassing), shoplifting food, and living out of doors in public parks or wooded areas. For those who spend significant amounts of time on the streets or going from shelter to shelter, this type of behavior is likely quite common.

"Social stigma occurs where there is unequal social, economic, and political power," said sociologist John R. Belcher of the University of Maryland. "It is an opportunity to label, stereotype, separate [us versus them], lose status, and discriminate."

Blame is primarily important to drunks and lawyers, often the same people. The ignorant and fearful blame the homeless person for being homeless, as if a factory bankruptcy closure is a moral failure by the delivery truck driver.

The root causes of people losing their homes, their jobs, their sense of identity, and any perks of social status are sudden or extended unemployment, limited affordable housing, mounting and unaffordable medical bills, and breakdowns in a broader support system of family and friends.[10]

A common stereotype of the homeless population is that they're all alcoholics or drug abusers. The truth is that a high percentage of homeless people do struggle with substance abuse, but it is often a result of homelessness, frequently arising after people lose their housing.

According to the National Coalition for the Homeless, "People who are homeless often turn to drugs and alcohol to

---

10. Comen, S., DeGaetano, A., Dhatt, Z., Duke, M., Flores, D., Jacques, T., Kaileh, L., Knight, K., Kushel, M., Ponder, K. Y., & Taylor, G. (2023). *Toward a New Understanding: The California Statewide Study of People Experiencing Homelessness*. University of California, San Francisco, Benioff Homelessness and Housing Initiative.

cope with their situations. They use substances in an attempt to attain temporary relief from their problems. Additionally, some people may view drug and alcohol use as necessary to be accepted among the homeless community."

Some use speed or crack to stay awake at night because falling asleep on the street would make them more vulnerable and more likely to be attacked.

The Coalition also notes that breaking an addiction is difficult for anyone, especially for the homeless. "To begin with, motivation to stop using substances may be poor. For many homeless people, survival is more important than personal growth and development, and finding food and shelter take a higher priority than drug counseling."

Many homeless people have also become estranged from their families and friends. Without a social support network, recovering from a substance addiction is very difficult.

Even if they do break their addictions, homeless people may have difficulty remaining sober while living on the streets where substances are so widely used.[11]

Unfortunately, many treatment programs focus on abstinence only programming, which is less effective than harm-reduction strategies and doesn't address the possibility of relapse (National Health Care for the Homeless Council, 2007).[12]

And then you have runaway teens such as Jimmy and Audrey. Like many troubled teens labeled as "different," they sought the geographical cure, imagining acceptance and becoming part of a more inclusive sub-culture.

Wrong.

11. Gary L. Fisher & Nancy A. Roget, eds., *Encyclopedia of Substance Abuse Prevention, Treatment, and Recovery* (Thousand Oaks, CA: SAGE Publications, 2009), https://sk.sagepub.com/ency/edvol/substance/chpt/homeless-substance-abuse-treatment.

12. National Health Care for the Homeless Council, "Addiction, Mental Health and Homelessness," 2007, www.nhchc.org.

For the mentally acute, there is a learning curve of only a few weeks for kids to become streetwise. They get hurt. They get ripped off. The ones with focused attention and social skills, at least to a superficial degree, make short work of that learning curve. Kitlas was blatantly bereft of focused attention, and pain-based learning curves repelled him immediately.

"That child," said Kelley, recognizing that Jimmy was honestly child-like, "responds to acceptance, inclusion, kindness—all things positive when provided with altruistic sincerity."

It was something akin to the "butterfly effect" that would ultimately change Jimmy's world. The basis of chaos theory, the butterfly effect poses the idea that a butterfly flapping its wings in Brazil can set off a hurricane in Texas. In Jimmy's world, that butterfly was a man named Daniel Patterson and the hurricane was Patterson's friendship with Meir Itaev.

MIDDLETOWN GRIT

Daniel Patterson, a rugged figure with close-cropped hair, is pushing 80 now, a devoted grandfather whose life story unfolds like a gritty novel ripped from the pages of the American underbelly.

He could easily pass for your unassuming neighbor, living quietly in a cozy suburban home nestled on a tree-lined street in a San Gabriel Valley town, just 15 miles east of the sprawling chaos of Los Angeles. For decades, this place has embodied the quintessential hallmarks of Middle America: an American flag-draped main street that waves patriotism like a banner in the wind, rows of charming mom-and-pop shops where locals swap stories over coffee, a worshipful devotion to the local high school football team that turns Friday nights into communal rituals, and an unyielding appreciation for the law enforcement officers who linger at Starbucks or the 7-Eleven, sipping free brews as guardians of the peace.

It is the kind of town where community bonds run deep, and Patterson's life here seems idyllic on the surface—a far cry from the whirlwind of schemes, scams, and survival that defined his younger years.

Patterson's home is a sanctuary of simple comforts, complete with a sparkling swimming pool that's essential for enduring those scorching Southern California days when the sun beats down like an unrelenting interrogator. He takes immense pride in the waist-high brick wall he constructed himself, brick by brick, often pointing it out with a grin as he strolls down the long driveway to haul in the trash cans.

His neighbors, meanwhile, inhabit what locals dub "McMansions"—towering remodels that sprawl across massive lots, soaring two or three stories high, crammed with luxurious cherrywood cabinets, gleaming marble countertops, and opulent entertainment rooms designed for Hollywood-style gatherings. Dan's abode, by contrast, retains the modest charm of a residence built in the 1980s or 1990s, unpretentious and lived-in, a testament to his grounded nature amid the surrounding extravagance.

As a doting grandfather to 23 grandchildren, his house buzzes with energy—kids darting in and out, family members from across the country dropping by for visits that fill the air with laughter and chaos. Step inside, and you're immediately greeted by Levi, his friendly, full-sized Dalmatian, whose wagging tail and eager eyes make every visitor feel like an old friend. The high-ceilinged hallway draws the eye upward to a stunning stained-glass window depicting Da Vinci's vision of the universe, through which morning sunlight pours in a radiant beam, cascading down the hall, illuminating the living room with its pristine ping pong table and spilling into the kitchen, where a sliding glass door opens to the inviting pool.

On chilly mornings, Dan stokes logs in the fireplace, creating a warm glow that contrasts with the constant hum of CNN in the background. His politics lean more liberal than his conservative neighbors, but in this spread-out town where homes are far apart yet everyone knows everyone's business, as long as you're friendly, ideologies fade into irrelevance. Friendliness is the currency here, and Dan trades generously in it.

Despite battling open-heart surgery and knee replacements that would sideline lesser men, Patterson remains remarkably fit, pounding the stadium steps daily at the high school across the street—a ritual that keeps his body sharp and his mind focused. He's an avid ping pong player, as evidenced by the immaculate table and paddles in the front room.

"I play against my grandson every day," Patterson boasts with a proud gleam in his eye, bending down to pet Levi, whose loyalty mirrors his owner's unyielding spirit. You get the unmistakable sense that Patterson rarely loses on that well-kept table; his competitive edge, honed over decades of high stakes living, ensures victory is almost a foregone conclusion.

It was in this very home, mere months after his arrest in an audacious failed gold scheme that shocked even seasoned investigators, that the FBI approached him with a proposition: wear a wire and help dismantle a dangerous drug dealer. Interviewing Patterson feels like engaging in a high-speed ping pong match—his stories volley back and forth with rapid-fire intensity, revealing a life crammed with colorful characters, both savory and unsavory. By his own account, he has lived a life brimming with adventure, rubbing shoulders with scholars, scoundrels, and everyone in between. His family tree boasts accomplished educators and intellectuals, and Dan fancies himself a teacher of sorts, imparting hard-won wisdom from the school of hard knocks.

Patterson's roots trace back to Muncie, Indiana, where he grew up in the shadow of Ball State University. In the early 20th century, natural gas discoveries transformed Muncie into a booming manufacturing hub, drawing jobs and prosperity. After World War II, it solidified as an industrial powerhouse, with giants like BorgWarner and Ball Glass establishing headquarters. Famously dubbed "Middletown, U.S.A." in a landmark 1940s sociological study, Muncie encapsulated the Midwest's essence: a town dominated by factories, where the rhythms of life pulsed to the beat of assembly lines, and power structures—from judges to the sheriff's department—were intertwined with industrial interests.[13]

"Yeah, Middletown," Patterson recalls with a nostalgic nod. "It was the heart of industrial America, where everything was controlled by that machine—jobs, politics, you name it."

Even into the 1940s and 1950s, the scars of the Civil War lingered in border states like Indiana, where Confederate sympathies simmered beneath the surface. It was still socially acceptable to embrace rebel heritage, and Dan's educated mother, hailing from West Virginia, proudly named her sons after Confederate generals.

"My brothers are David Jackson, Douglas Lee, and I'm Daniel Crance—after General William Rosecrans," Dan notes, his voice carrying a mix of amusement and reflection. Love for the Confederacy existed on a spectrum, from benign naming traditions to outright hatred toward Blacks, Catholics, and Jews. For decades, the Ku Klux Klan loomed large in Muncie, its members infiltrating positions of power, organizing rallies and marches that poisoned the community. In nearby Marion, lynchings of Black youth were grim realities, and Klan supporters flaunted their bigotry openly.

Shockingly, Dan's second-grade teacher displayed Klan memorabilia in her classroom—a mask and symbols that served as a chilling backdrop to lessons. "I remember she had a mask and one of the symbols," Patterson says. "But that wasn't me. I was an athlete. I was exposed to Black people, and I liked them. We played together, competed together."

Until the 1970s, Muncie's political machine was a cesspool of corruption, run by men who fleeced taxpayers through bid rigging, kickbacks, sweetheart deals, and cronyism—schemes that rarely faced consequences. Yet, amid the Klan's shadow and graft, Muncie boasted diversity,

---

13. Lynd, H. M., Lynd, R. S. (1929). *Middletown: A Study in American Culture.* United Kingdom: Harcourt, Brace.

as documented in Ball State's Oral History Project. Jobs were plentiful for those willing to work, provided they adhered to the rigid lines of segregation.

"The dividing line in town was McCullough Park—one side Black, our side White," Patterson explains. The Black neighborhood, known as Whitely, consisted mostly of housing projects and was notorious for its roughness.

"It was a tough town—lots of drinking, lots of fighting. In high school, I'd sneak into their nightclubs, play poker at Tish's Chicken Shack." Tish's was one of two all-night juke joints in Muncie, the other slinging pork chops, both vying for a crowd of young revelers with cash to burn and a taste for all-night parties.

"You'd go to one and stay until dawn," recalls a local from the era. "They were straight out of the movies—like the club in Little Richard's life story, his dad's spot. Not quite as rough, but close."

At just 16, fresh out of high school, Dan bolted for Hawaii, craving adventure beyond Muncie's confines. "I went over to Hawaii, living with a kid from Northern Illinois. We did everything—Hawaii wasn't the tourist trap it is today."

Poverty hit hard; he parked cars at The Red Rooster restaurant, hating every minute, surviving like a beach bum—waking in the sand, surfing endlessly. Fate intervened when he met a young friend whose dad ran a salvage ship for Matson Steamship Line. "He got me a job on that ship, and I took it." Thus began a nomadic odyssey across the South Pacific—Japan, Vietnam, Northern Africa, Casablanca, Tunisia—before looping back. On a Mariana Islands beach, introspection struck. "You ain't gonna do this all your life." Returning to Hawaii, he flew home, landing in Burbank, hitchhiking to Muncie. College beckoned—Ball State initially, but Purdue wooed him for football.

Like a real-life Forrest Gump, Dan's speed on the field earned him a scholarship at Purdue during the Boilermakers'

Big Ten dominance. He said he played alongside quarterback Bob Griese, shining enough to travel to Los Angeles for the Rose Bowl—his first taste of the West Coast glamor. The record books say it didn't happen, but Dan insists it did. He tells a good story.

But celebration back home turned tragic: a random drive-by shooting outside a popular restaurant on the wrong side of town shattered his dreams, ending his football career and rerouting his path. Dan turned to academia, earning a master's in geology and even teaching briefly, but Muncie pulled him back like a magnet.

Recounting one visit, he rolls up his sleeve to reveal a scar. "I walked into a bar on Eighth Street in Muncie, got past the stamp check, and bam—a guy stabs me in the arm. The knife stuck, so I yanked it out and stabbed him in the shoulder. Survival mode."

Soon, Dan dove into union organizing for the Garment Workers Union, rallying sweatshop workers from Ohio to West Virginia. It was grueling, high-tension work where tempers flared—workers demanding better pay and benefits clashing with profit-hungry owners. Dan roared in behind the wheel of his 1972 Chevy Monte Carlo, a chocolate-brown muscle car with a black vinyl top, emblematic of American power at its peak. In the late 1960s and early 1970s Rust Belt, civil unrest boiled over, trigger-happy cops patrolled, and union agitators were persona non grata in company towns.

"I carried a double-barreled shotgun under the seat, double-ought buck, triggers wired together," he recalls with a steely gaze. "You never know on these campaigns—some end in violence. Better to have it than not. Came through Dayton one night; I'm sure I'd be dead without it."

The job demanded cunning: identifying plant leaders and collecting union cards for NLRB elections, all while dodging company smear campaigns. "It got tough," Dan admits. "Companies ran hit jobs on you." One night in

Kentucky, exhausted from a drive, he napped in his car with a .357 Magnum on his chest. A familiar cop, Jack, tapped the window. "Dan, what's going on?"

"Just protection," Dan replied. No ticket—just a nod from a lifelong acquaintance.

During this era, Dan crossed paths with Bobby Vesco, a financier linked to Richard Nixon. "Unions organize anybody," Dan explains. He unionized Vesco's Pennsylvania tool and die shop, earning the man's initial hatred—but friendship followed. That was before Vesco's infamous "thing": amassing millions through a dummy company, Overseas Investment Corporation, during the oil crisis, siphoning funds from banks like Bundesbank and Chase. Much of it fueled Nixon's 1972 reelection and the Watergate break-in. Indicted with Nixon's Attorney General John Mitchell and Secretary of Commerce Maurice Stans, Vesco fled to Costa Rica on a stolen jet, battling extradition with local government aid.

Years later, Vesco's aide, Norman LeBlanc—a gaunt, pale man in a light gray suit—tracked Dan down. "Bob wants you to work for him. Here's $2,000. Buy a ticket to Costa Rica." Intrigued, Dan flew south, meeting Costa Rica's president (later ousted amid Vesco scandals). Vesco offered him a bodyguard role: "I trust you."

Escorted to Vesco's ranch, guarded by 50 Costa Rican soldiers, Dan bonded over fishing on Vesco's 135-foot yacht, *The Zodiac*, armed with a 50-caliber machine gun and surface-to-air missiles.

"I liked the guy," Dan confesses. But when asked why Vesco risked it all, the reply was chilling. "Dan, I just wanted to see if it could be done."

Vesco's influence extended far. "He had Agnew down in the Bahamas getting blowjobs from the natives." But U.S. pressure forced Vesco out. "When the U.S. sneezes, Costa Rica catches a cold," Dan muses wistfully.

By the mid-1970s, Dan shed his violent past—"I'm nonviolent now, got rid of my guns"—and towed his Monte Carlo to California. Union ties landed him at GM's Southgate plant, but ambition called. Leveraging his geology degree, he joined Occidental Petroleum in Los Angeles as a strategic planner under CEO Armand Hammer, trading commodities, overseeing the Knoedler Art Gallery in New York, and managing global lithium mines. The gig was short-lived; one day, Dan marched into Hammer's office. "I'm quitting. Starting a mining company in Mexico." Hammer's response was, "What are you gonna do?" Dan's bold reply sealed it.

In Mexico City, success surged with a tungsten mine, but government mandates required a 51% Mexican partner. As production boomed, demands escalated while pursuing contracts with State-owned steel firms. Triumph turned terror: at the airport, a week before Easter, a Uzi pressed to his head, a revolver in his side. Airport police intervened, but his partner was kidnapped for ransom. Dan's first FBI encounter proved lifesaving; grateful, he fled back to L.A.

Undeterred, Dan launched a carbon recycling business that ballooned into a multi-million-dollar juggernaut. "I had a big operation going," he says. Selling it to his son (who runs it in Indiana), Dan retreated to Costa Rica, establishing an offshore sports book. "Bought property in the free zone, set up Blue Parrot Sports with computers galore. Ran ads in Lindy's magazine." A *New York Times* exposé on U.S.-backed Costa Rican books killed the venture.

Bouncing around, Dan frequented Plummer Park, where he met Meir "Mike" Itaev, a scam virtuoso. "Mike was the master," Dan recalls. Itaev's crew stole corporate checks, cashing them through proxies. Mike eyed a $75,000 UPS check, but Dan waved it off. "Too risky—works once, then you're burned." Their bond sparked over Dan's Viagra prescription; Mike bought 30 pills, gifting designer jeans in return.

Soon, Mike visited Dan's home. "If you can get more Viagra, let me know." Dan's savvy was, "Think big, set up a phony distributor, buy cases from pharmacies." Mike executed the plan, hauling 20 cases from one, 10 from another. "Beautiful idea," Mike praised him.

DR. CHARLES SCHULTZ

Dan's friendship with Mike took off from there. Mike introduced Dan to his friends, and Dan shared his intuitive knowledge of corporate operations.

"Yeah. I mean, I've been a corporate person all my life. So, I know the intricacies of how companies operate," Dan recalls, thinking back on his early days working with Mike on a lucrative gold scam.

"And I passed that on to Mike. I could go to any company in the world, and I can tell you how they operate. From the financial part to the back office."

Mike and Dan thought if they could scam drug companies out of Viagra, maybe they could scam bigger companies out of something more valuable—like gold.

So, how did it work?

"Well, I built the stories but didn't make the call," Dan said.

"Uh, you know, we're Ball Corporation or some other big vendor that would use gold. And we would order it and give them a PO and everything. It could have been anybody. The story's pretty good for anything, as long as you know what they use the gold for and that they have dealt with the company before.

"You've got to be smart enough to know where the gold is being used. I told Mike we could use this story and buy gold wire or sheet gold that was ninety-four to ninety-nine percent pure."

One such scam involved conning gold from a dental manufacturer and impressively pocketing about $200,000 in an afternoon. Mike took the first few shipments to a pawn shop in Hollywood. The friend had the shop out front and a fence operation in the back. There he would melt the gold.

Mike and Dan would also take the raw gold to the Jewelry District in downtown Los Angeles. Mike had a contact on the third floor of a building at 6th and Hill.

"Sometimes we couldn't cash it because it was too much. When it sold, I would get a percentage," Dan said, adding with pride. "I was the brains of that gold operation."

A light bulb eventually went off in Dan's head. What if they moved the operation to Pasadena and claimed to be military officers affiliated with JPL or Caltech?

Scientists attached to Caltech have won 41 Nobel prizes, including nine for Chemistry and 18 for Physics. Caltech has helped manage space explorations, including the Mars Rover, the two Voyager probes, and dozens of other contributions to our scientific knowledge of the universe.

Because the Pasadena-based agencies manage most of the Earth-orbiting satellites, their affiliation with the Department of Defense goes back generations—all the way to the discovery of atomic power and the development of the atom bomb. That legacy is on full display as Albert Einstein's papers are housed just off campus.

So, when the Boston-based firm now known as LeachGarner received a phone call from a man identifying himself as Sergeant Michael Jefferies, a defense procurement expert seeking gold for a "neutron accelerator project" in Pasadena, few eyebrows, if any, were raised. On its website, the company explains what it does and how it serves the government:

"LeachGarner is a precious metals supplier to the United States government market leveraging our wire, tubing, sheet, and casting grain capabilities... supplying quality precious metal coin blanks to multiple public and private mints. Coin blanks are available in mill finish or burnished finish. LeachGarner offers multiple qualities of gold, silver, platinum, and palladium alloys for our blank production."

Reading between the lines on the website, it turns out all of the U.S. gold isn't in Fort Knox; there's lots in Massachusetts. Like all good wholesale house sales reps, whoever took the call from "Jefferies" asked for a purchase order.

An official-looking Department of Defense purchase order came via fax two days later.

Return address on the paperwork showed it came from the Defense Finance and Accounting System, or DFAS, the federal agency that pays contractors out of its nearly $1 trillion annual budget.

If you're scamming the government, DFAS is a good place to start. DFAS accountants once paid $14,000 for individual 3-D printed toilet seat lids and bought cups for $1,280 each. Weird purchases from DFAS are notorious, including $436 for hammers in the 1980s, and $117 soap dish covers and $999 pliers in the 1990s.

This "requisition order" from Jefferies to Leach from DFAS simply asked for gold—and didn't seek to overpay for it. The order also had some very specific instructions. It asked that the gold be delivered to the "Jet Propulsion Laboratories (JPL), Assembly Research Division, Pasadena, CA."—Neutron Accelerator project.

Two things about it immediately drew questions from sharp eyes in the gold vendor's office.

Despite an official-looking seal, the order didn't look like anything else they had ever received from the government, plus Sgt. Jefferies had misspelled his own title "Sargent" instead of "Sergeant."

The $1.6 million in gold would be shipped to the Neutron Accelerator Research Building located on North San Gabriel Boulevard in Pasadena, Unit 103. Jefferies asked that the gold be addressed there in care of Dr. Charles Schultz—a man who coincidentally shared a name with the cartoonist responsible for the creation of the *Peanuts* comic strip.

When they were quizzed more deeply about the purchase order, the men claimed that they were also working on a top secret project for the space shuttle.

If Google Earth had been available, the Sterns salesman would easily have ascertained that the "lab" was in a rundown office park on the east end of Pasadena, far from Caltech. This dump was anything but a top secret government lab. Truth be told, the place would be a better fit for a meth lab or an indoor pot grow.

Jefferies explained to the salesman that the office wasn't outfitted with a telephone, so any calls to Schultz would have to be via cell phone. "The laboratory where Dr. Schultz works is under construction and does not have any telephone lines," Jefferies said, adding that the need for high-quality gold was immediate.

"Deliver this gold as soon as you can; it's going on the shuttle," Jefferies explained.

"How are you paying for this?" the salesman wanted to know.

"We'll send you a check from the Department of Defense as soon as it's delivered," was the reply.

Knowing that the Department of Defense had switched to electronic funds transfers and hadn't written a check in months, the Sterns salesman called his bosses, who called the Department of Defense. An investigation commenced.

In Washington, DC, the Department of Defense managed detectives around the country who tracked down the con men involved in fraud cases. These guys weren't playing.

Special Agent Jim Houghlin was assigned the task of hunting down "Sgt. Jefferies" and "Dr. Schultz."

A special agent with the Department of Defense Office (DOD) of the Inspector General, Defense Criminal Investigative Service (DCIS) in Boston, Houghlin conducted numerous investigations involving crime in Department of Defense programs, including healthcare fraud, money laundering, public corruption, and corruption in the federal procurement process.

Many of his cases concerned what are known as Special Access Programs (SAP) or breaches involving top secret and classified intelligence. Houghlin's investigations often led to criminal convictions, multi-million-dollar civil settlements, and large asset seizures.

One of his probes involved the Systems Management American Corporation out of Norfolk, Virginia, where the corporate bigwigs put together a RICO-level scam that cost the U.S. Navy millions, if not billions of dollars. The investigation uncovered conspiracy to defraud the U.S. government, public corruption, and obstruction of justice.

Another investigation instigated by Jim at DCIS resulted in the arrests of a brother and sister who were scamming the Army on sole source contracts. That investigation earned Houghlin the Department of Justice Award for Public Service.

Because they provided an address, catching up with Jefferies and Schultz proved easy. All Houghlin had to do was follow the shipment to the receivers.

December 21, 2000, was a perfect Southern California day to be on a stakeout for an arrest. Temperatures hovered in the 60s, and the feds prepared an armored car to make their "delivery."

As law enforcement approached the neighborhood, it was clear that some counter surveillance was in effect. Two guys, who obviously didn't belong there, were circling the block and eyeing the fake JPL location.

The task force got eyeballs on them and set up a tail before going in. A group of investigators warily approached the "lab." It was Houghlin who knocked on the door of the office, purporting to be affiliated with JPL. A sign at eye level plainly said, "Neutron Accelerator Lab." A youngish man with a slight accent and wearing a lab coat that clearly identified him as Dr. Charles Schultz came to the door.

"Can you sign for the gold?" Houghlin asked, as he pointed to a crate with gold sheets and wire ordered by someone at the lab.

"Yes, of course."

"Same name as the *Peanuts* comic guy," someone remarked as Schultz took out a pen to sign for the shipment.

"I get that all the time," Lab Coat Guy responded.

"Not for long," came the reply. "You are under arrest."

Handcuffed and arrested were Anthony M. Macaluso, 19, and Alexander "Dr. Schultz" Drabkin, 42.

Daniel Patterson and Mike Itaev were outside, scouting the drop-off. Both were also detailed. Despite their arrests in Pasadena, Mike and Dan were soon back out on the street.

A few days later, Mike introduced Dan to Alex Proctor, a guy wanted Dan's help getting rid of a pesky reporter.

As Proctor explained, *L.A. Times* reporter Anita Busch was digging up dirt on actor Steven Seagal, the star of several action movies.

Seagal's business partner was Hollywood super-agent Michael Ovitz. A private investigator named Anthony Pellicano, known as the PI to the stars, asked Alex to do some work for him.

Alex explained that he owed Pellicano $14,000, and getting Busch out of the way would settle the debt. As Alex saw it, they needed to send a message to the reporter—

possibly even kill her. It's not clear what was in it for Dan and Meir.

This was no joke. Dan realized Proctor was as serious and as dangerous as any man he had ever met. Gambling and drugs were one thing. Murder was something else, and Dan's mind was racing. He knew he would be having no part of the plan.

Alex explained that he had cased Busch's apartment and considered setting her car on fire. The only problem with that was the possibility of setting the carport on fire and, by extension, the entire apartment building where she lived.

Too risky.

So, he settled on a simpler approach.

A few days after the meeting in the Russian bortsch palace, LAPD detectives received a phone call from Busch. The reporter had gone out to her car that morning and noticed a note taped to the windshield that said: "STOP."

Once they targeted the reporter, Dan knew he had to get out.

Just below the note, the windshield was shattered as if punctured by a bullet or projectile. Almost like putting a bow on the message, there was also a dead fish with a rose in its mouth staring through the busted window glass.

LAPD called the bomb squad and Busch went into hiding.

Dan called Alex and told him, "I'm not into that."

The next day, Busch received a warning call from Dan.

Dan figured he owed nothing to Itaev or Proctor.

"So, I called down to Anita. It took me a while to get a hold of her. And I kept saying, 'I have an extremely important message that needs to be given in person.'"

Dan says he and Busch connected later that day.

"And I said, 'Anita, you are in danger. This is not a threat call. I'm trying to help. You're in danger. I don't care if you tap my phone call. I'm not trying to get you to hide or anything. I just want you to know you need some help.' And she called the FBI that night."

The FBI wasted no time. Within hours, agents were sitting at Dan's kitchen table, grilling him about Proctor, Pellicano, their connection to Busch, and the plot to kill her. Dan gave up Proctor, but the agents wanted more. They wanted Dan to wear a wire and draw Proctor out—find out how connected he was to Pellicano, drug dealing, and celebrity mischief.

Dan wore a wire to every subsequent meeting with Alex. Agents followed them everywhere. Eventually, in November 2002, Proctor was arrested, and so was Pellicano.

About the same time as the arrests of Proctor and Pellicano, Mier "Mike" Itaev was taken into custody, although the circumstances were different. Agents bagged Mike in connection with the conspiracy to import and distribute the drug MDMA, commonly known as "ecstasy" or "Molly."

Mike pled guilty, was sentenced to federal prison, and was there as the butterfly effect of the caper resulted in the murder of Aleks Markzitser in June 2004.

BUTTERFLIES ARE FREE TO FLY

With Mike Itaev in custody, his nephew Mark Itaev and brother Gary Itaev needed a plan to secure Mike's release.

The strategy was complex, audacious, and inherently risky, relying on deception and requiring the expertise of someone with deep knowledge and high-level contacts within the federal government.

They turned to Mike's attorney, an individual with the necessary qualifications to navigate such a scheme.

On the night Markzitser was killed, the West Hollywood Sheriff's Substation received a 9-1-1 call from her.

The attorney reported the homicide, providing precise details about the location of the body and the suspects involved. The deputy listening took note as the attorney clarified the reason for calling.

She explained that the call was on behalf of clients who were working as informants for the DEA and, after consulting with the clients' handler, the attorney was instructed to contact the authorities.

Mark and Gary had entered into an agreement with federal authorities, including the DEA and FBI, in the summer of 2003, serving as confidential informants.[14]

---

14. Patrick James Kitlas, Notice of Motion Requesting Court to Hold 28 U.S.C. § 2254 Habeas Corpus Petition in Abeyance Pending Exhaustion of State Court Claims/Remedies (and Authorities in Support Thereof), No. CV 08-6359-ABC (AJW), Cent. Dist. Cal., Sept. 28, 2008.

As such, they provided valuable information to law enforcement[15], leading to the apprehension of fugitives in Glendale and San Diego. Mike Itaev, however, held a deep contempt for informants.

Though he was reportedly also designated as a confidential informant, Mike never provided information to authorities, likely due to his longstanding aversion to cooperating in such a manner.

Confidential informants, as explained by a noted Hollywood security expert, Fred Wolfson, typically fall into two categories, each driven by distinct motivations. These individuals often face significant legal pressures, compelling them to share information about criminal activities to mitigate their own consequences.

According to Wolfson, snitches are those who are working off an arrest or criminal charge, and those non-criminal busybodies who believe they're performing a public service every time they drop a dime on notoriously powerless prostitutes or low-level neighborhood drug dealers.

"The motives for snitching," Wolfson said, "are always self-serving. The busted criminal is looking for a better deal or a get out of jail free card; the public-spirited cop-caller is a law enforcement groupie whose snitching gives them a sense of positive purpose."

Occasionally, of course, anti-snitching efforts are themselves the cause of suspicion and arrest. In October 2016, the pleasant and attractive April Lynn Lavender was arrested and charged with felony possession of a controlled substance with intent to deliver after she posted a sign on her front door: "Due to snitches, everyone entering my home is subject to being searched. All cell phones and drinks will be

---

15. Patrick James Kitlas & Mark Itayev, Petition for Review, No. S158755 (B187855), Sup. Ct. Cal., filed following Ct. App. decision July 23, 2007, Los Angeles Super. Ct. No. SA053282-0.

left outside. If you're not a snitch, it won't offend you if I search you."

Because of the sign, police received consent to search the home, where substantial quantities of heroin and methamphetamine were found.[16]

"While drug investigations often require a great deal of time and effort," said Fayette County Sheriff Steve Kessler, "sometimes the criminals make our job easy. If someone posts a sign on their front door about searching 'snitches,' it's a pretty safe bet that there are illegal drugs being sold out of that location."

Defense attorney Leslie Ballin has seen both sides of informants. He has represented those who decide to become confidential informants and has worked against informants, testifying against his clients. Accustomed to the spotlight, Balin's cases have appeared on media outlets such as CourtTV, CNN, *Nancy Grace*, *The Larry King Show*, and *The Oprah Winfrey Show*. The firm's attorneys are routinely seen on local news channels representing clients throughout the Midsouth.

"Once you draw that line and become an informant, then you're supposed to live a law-abiding life. Truth of the matter is that really isn't the case, and I believe law enforcement at times turns a blind eye to what their informants are doing in the street," said Ballin.

"When you're arrested," retired diamond heist mastermind Pavle "Punch" Stanimirovic explained, "they do their best to turn you into a snitch right away. If I had turned rat on my father and all our associates, I could have walked free. The arrest would simply disappear as if it never existed. Everyone else goes to prison; I walk free. I would never, could never do that. If I did, I would have had a book deal decades ago and I would have been famous already.

---

16. "Sign Posted on Front Door Leads to Drug Arrest in Fayette County," WCHSTV.com, https://wchstv.com/news/local/sign-posted-on-front-door-leads-to-drug-arrest-in-fayette-county.

Who wants to be called a rat? I never was a rat. People hate rats. Hell, Ken Eurell was a dirty cop, but more people are mad at him because they think he turned rat on Michael Dowd, his dirty cop partner. The truth doesn't matter to most people. Ken never was a rat, but people think he snitched. He didn't, but he still gets hate mail."

The DEA relies on essentially unreliable self-serving accusations of "snitches" who wouldn't mind at all planting mannitol-cut California cocaine on Calcutta's Mother Teresa or stuffing AK-47s in the luggage of the Mormon Tabernacle Choir for an upcoming shoot-out in the southwest if doing so were to their perceived legal or financial advantage.

The "best snitches" are street-level sex workers in countries or counties where sex work is illegal. Their law enforcement contact will get them excluded from prosecution when they're arrested in a sweep or find themselves arrested for a singular act of professional indiscretion.

Snitches work at all levels, from street crime to corporate boardrooms.

Confidential informants aren't the same as whistle blowers, although a whistleblower may become a C.I.

As these high-level informants primarily reveal corrupt, illegal behavior, there are supposedly laws in place to protect them. Don't count on it.

A police officer who discovered that five individuals were railroaded for a murder they didn't commit bravely championed their release. Hailed as a hero of justice, he was nonetheless denied his pension because in revealing the false arrest and prosecution of these innocents, he violated city policy against disclosing confidential information.

"The difference between the snitch and the whistleblower," remarked Fred Wolfson, "is that the snitch is selfish, and the whistleblower isn't."

Some would say snitches snitch as a matter of rational self-interest.

"In all my years, I've never had an informant doing it because they were a concerned citizen," said Salt Lake Police Intelligence Detective Ron "Racer" Nelson, who added that informants generally only have information about the bad guys because he or she is on the inside.

Court documents show that Mark and Gary Itaev were confidential informants for the federal Drug Enforcement Administration.[17]

As Mark saw it, the DEA had a sliding scale for cooperation, creating the expectation that if he informed on a big enough crime, the result would be Mike Itaev's release from federal custody.[18]

One crime big enough to fit the bill was murder.

In the murky world of confidential informants, rules are meant to govern their actions, ensuring accountability and oversight. Yet, with Mark, those regulations were cast aside, raising questions about law enforcement's adherence to protocol.

Established in 2001 under then-Attorney General Janet Reno, the U.S. Department of Justice's Guidelines Regarding the Use of Confidential Informants are explicit: "Illegal activity by a confidential informant must be authorized in advance and in writing for a specified period, not to exceed 90 days."

These guidelines, designed to prevent abuse and maintain control over informants' activities, require regular oversight and documentation. There isn't a lot of documentation about the Itaevs or the totality of their interactions with law enforcement.

---

17. Patrick James Kitlas & Mark Itaev, Petition for Review, No. S158755 (B187855), Sup. Ct. Cal., filed following Ct. App. decision July 23, 2007, Los Angeles Super. Ct. No. SA053282-01.

18. Patrick James Kitlas, Notice of Motion Requesting Court to Hold 28 U.S.C. § 2254 Habeas Corpus Petition in Abeyance Pending Exhaustion of State Court Claims/Remedies (and Authorities in Support Thereof), No. CV 08-6359-ABC (AJW), Cent. Dist. Cal., Sept. 28, 2008. In custody interview of Mark Itaev.

Regardless, Mark knew that any time he met with the police, he held some chips. His interactions with a man known only as "Shadow" and his pregnant girlfriend went unmonitored by any law enforcement agency, local or federal, sources familiar with the case confirmed.

The absence of oversight left Itaev free to operate in a legal gray zone, with no apparent checks on his actions.

And Mark was deep in the program by the time June rolled around. Even though he had avoided problems following his check washing arrests, his uncle was in custody and needed to be freed.

TOUGH GUY

On June 7, 2004, Audrey and Jimmy planned to spend the night at the C & C Internet Café.

"It was open twenty-four/seven," he recalled. "I mostly played *Counterstrike* and looked up *Star Wars* stuff. It was well-lit. The food was cheap and good. And we had a good rapport with the staff."

A group of guys usually hung around the entryway selling speed and ketamine to the patrons who intended to stay up all night playing games and socializing on MySpace or in AOL chat rooms.

In other parts of the world, internet cafés housed terrorists, seditionists, and troublemakers. In Hollywood, most such cafés were utilized by addicts, dealers, and the young homeless like Audrey and Jimmy. Many were open 24 hours.

At $8.00 an hour to rent a cubicle, a three- or four-hour stay was conceivably cheaper than a Hollywood Boulevard motel and most nights, you could overstay your welcome without much trouble.

Some accommodated visitors with pool tables, televisions, all-night coffee service, and live music.

Shadow, who liked the food there, hardly ever paid for the entertainment. He mostly deemed the venue as a place to get off the street.

"I knew everyone there," he said. "Even the gangbangers." By 9:00 p.m., the management had enough of Jimmy and so had local gang members who erroneously assumed that he knew the phone number of a bicycle-riding speed dealer encroaching on their territory.

"I kept telling them that I didn't know the guy or his phone number, but they didn't believe me. Well, I got out of there, and Audrey was about an hour behind, but we stayed near the entrance and as temperatures dropped, we planned on ways to get back inside," Kitlas recalled.

Around midnight, an old boyfriend of Audrey's came by and invited her to stay at the home of a mutual acquaintance. Audrey said the friend, whom she only knew as "Gia," was hosting a small get-together.

It was about then, leaving for the party, that Shadow noticed a cool black pickup truck.

"I have always liked pickup trucks, so I noticed it right away," he recalled. "The weird thing was that it seemed to be following us because when we left the so-called get-together, there it was again. It was, like, circling the block or something."

Almost immediately after arriving, Audrey realized the party wasn't her scene.

"It was mostly Mafia guys and that wasn't her thing because she didn't speak the language, so she was put out of place because of it," Jimmy recalled. "There was about maybe ten or twenty people there, I think."

Feeling like she did, Audrey convinced Jimmy to leave. The couple went outside and started walking, looking for a comfortable place to spend the night. They wound up on Sierra Bonita, the street where Markzitser lived.

"The corner lot had a big front lawn, and we sat down under a tree," Jimmy recalled. "I have a thing about spiders, and I was concerned that a spider was going to show up. Instead, it was that same big black truck circling the block, and Mark Itaev coming around the corner. He doesn't seem all that surprised to see us, you know, it's just a happy coincidence. He starts telling me that he has something for me. There is an apartment that he can arrange for me to take over and live in and pay the rent. I didn't understand how that could work, but he said he would explain it."

Jimmy said he didn't know where Mark lived, but he assumed it was nearby because Mark had his dog with him.

"Just about then, this other guy comes walking up from the other direction. I don't know him, but Audrey recognizes him because she says that she's met him before. She called him Sasha. He's obviously tipsy and he recognizes Mark right away like they are old pals or something, and he invites Mark to come to his place for a few drinks. They start walking up Sierra Bonita and Audrey has to pee, so she kinda runs after them and asks if she can use his bathroom. Mark says a few words to him in Russian, and the guy says okay, and she goes to use the bathroom."

Itaev ran back to get Audrey. Jimmy decided to stay put. Audrey, Mark, and Sasha then walked fast up the street to Markzitser's apartment.

Once Audrey finished in the bathroom, Sasha wanted to know if she was hungry. The couple talked for about 20 minutes while she ate.

Throughout the interlude, a separate conversation was going on in Russian between Mark and Sasha, with the inebriated host casting continual glances at Audrey.

Itaev explained to Audrey that Sasha wanted to buy some booze. As they were leaving, Audrey reached for her backpack, which held her life's most precious items—clothing and CDs.

"Leave it here," Itaev said. "We'll be back."

At that, they left the apartment and walked down the street to where they had left Jimmy.

As they approached, Audrey broke out in a run, grabbing Jimmy and pulling him toward her, and she laid a big kiss on his lips.

By the time Mark and Sasha arrived, tongues were being exchanged, and the couple's hands were all over one another. Sasha started yelling at Itaev in Russian. Itaev tried to calm him down, but it was no use.

Jimmy had a rudimentary understanding of Russian, but he didn't hear what was said.

Nonetheless, Sasha drunkenly stormed off. He had anticipated sex with Audrey. She had no previous inclination, but at that moment, and by her own later admission, she knew two things: The couple needed a place to stay, and with the gangbangers from the internet café still looking for Jimmy and hoping to have him hook them up with the bike-riding speed dealer, the street situation on Sierra Bonita was becoming increasingly uncomfortable.

Standing on the sidewalk after Sasha had left them, Mark, Audrey, and Jimmy talked about how they might get back into his apartment and spend the night.

They at least needed to return to get Audrey's backpack.

"I wasn't so sure it would be that easy," Jimmy recalled. "I told Mark that I wasn't confident that Sasha would let me in—especially because Sasha was pissed that he wasn't going to be able to have sex with Audrey."

"I figured that Mark and Sasha had a separate agreement about Audrey—maybe Mark promised she would sleep with Sasha if he allowed them to stay. It was unclear, but I wanted nothing to do with getting into the apartment, especially if it meant getting into an argument over Audrey. That's when Mark began taunting me."

"Aren't you a man? Go in there and knock him out," Mark urged. "You can take over the apartment and begin making the payments so you can live here and take care of Audrey, and the baby you guys are going to have."

According to the young couple, the taunts became bolder.

"You don't have the balls to do this. Come on, man, you could come up big here," Mark continued. "Show me you can do this."

At some point, Jimmy decided he couldn't stand Mark being so in his face.

"I figured at least I could go in and grab the backpack. I was afraid of Mark because I had seen him threaten people and hurt them, and he had even threatened me a few times. Mark wanted me to knock Sasha out, tie him up, take his valuables, and take over his payments, his rent, and the entire apartment. Mark said that they could steal the man's identity. I worried that something would happen to Audrey and the baby if I didn't follow through. I headed over to the apartment. Audrey wasn't far behind me."

When Jimmy got inside, the first thing he did was secure Audrey's backpack.

"*Spasiba*," Jimmy said, using his best Russian for "thank you." He wanted to prove to Mark he was tough. Then and there, he decided to act. Having done some high school wrestling, Jimmy held confidence in only one move, and he used it. A surprise headlock on the older and drunken Sasha brought him crashing down.

Outside, Audrey was concerned that it was taking Shadow too long to get her backpack, so she came to the apartment and walked in the unlocked door just as her boyfriend was hogtying Sasha with a wire or cord that had been yanked out of the wall.

When she saw that, she was furious and gave him hell for doing something so stupid.

"She was terribly upset by what she saw and stormed out," said Kitlas. "I sat on the floor and cried."

Lane, returning to Itaev, told him what she had seen, refused to go back up there, and watched as Mark went to join Kitlas in Sasha's apartment.

Once inside, Mark ransacked the apartment while barking orders at Jimmy, telling him to untie the drunken

Sasha and put him on the bed. The two men untied Sasha together.

Mark instructed Jimmy to take certain things from Sasha's apartment, which he did.

"At all times while in the presence of Sasha, he was always alive and breathing, even when he was placed in his bed after Mark assured me that he would sleep everything off since he was drunk, which Itaev also made sure of prior to introducing him to me."

Jimmy was convinced that Mark also held Sasha's keys.

After telling Jimmy what items to take from the apartment, Itaev left and returned to the corner.

There, according to Audrey, Mark said Sasha was dead, and that Jimmy had killed him. He told her that he was worried that the police would show up at any minute. He had no alibi. She had no alibi. But they could both blame Jimmy for the killing as a way to get out from being under suspicion.

He told her that if the police asked about the crime, she should tell them that she and Itaev had nothing to do with it.

It was getting colder outside as the night wore on, and the coastal fog began to roll in. Soon, Audrey and Mark were joined by Jimmy, who was wearing a jacket he had taken from the apartment. He was also carrying a laptop and its case. When he had left, he locked the door of the bedroom.

Once they were together again, Mark said he would meet them in 15 minutes at a 7-Eleven on nearby Santa Monica Boulevard.

The couple took off for the 7-Eleven. Mark apparently returned to Aleks's apartment to use the telephone but found the bedroom door locked from the inside. After all, it is known that Mark used Aleks's cordless phone to report the murder, and that could only happen after Jimmy was no longer there.

Audrey later recalled that Itaev seemed panicked, high strung, out of breath and agitated when he rejoined them.

He said he had to leave again and get his dog out of Aleks's apartment and then he would return to the convenience store.

"Things just got stranger because we waited for Mark at the store and he didn't come back," recalled Jimmy, "so I decided to go back to up to Sierra Bonita and look for him. Well, you know damn well what the first thing I notice is that same black pickup truck coming down the street and, guess what? This time it stops and out of it comes Mark! That just messed with my head big time."

Once inside the pickup, Jimmy saw Mark's dog was there too.

The dog, a big, white part-Pitbull puppy named Arazi, was rambunctious most of the time, but in the truck he was subdued. Mark introduced the driver, Gary, as his "friend," and they began to drive toward Santa Monica Boulevard, just north of Sasha's apartment. That's when Jimmy began to object.

"What about Audrey?" He convinced them to turn around and go to the convenience store, where Audrey was still waiting.

After picking up the girl, they began to drive, stopping a few minutes later at the Hollywood Econo Lodge.

The motel, painted a garish shade of pink, was adorned with a neon sign and a large mural depicting a pair of movie cameras, a five-pointed star, and some palm trees.

It might have been the perfect setting for the out-of-towner hoping to experience some magic as long as they ignored the pawn shop, the check cashing business, and a chain sandwich shop across the street. At the time, Econo Lodge was one of several pay-by-the-hour Hollywood haunts that served hookers, dopers, and outcasts. It was a good place to lie low.

When they pulled up, Gary Itaev hopped out and went to the desk, where he paid for a room. He made sure Audrey and Jimmy were situated before leaving with Mark.

Not far behind the group was the police. When they arrived, the officers were met by Mark and Gary.

Mark explained that they were holding Jimmy and Audrey at the hotel because the couple had murdered and robbed a man in West Hollywood.

He claimed that Jimmy had learned that the dead man wanted to sleep with Audrey and Jimmy was jealous. Mark said that he, Kitlas, and Lane were staying at the motel in a room Gary had rented for them.

Gary said he was only involved to help his brother Mike Itaev, who was in federal custody at the time. He believed that because a murder had occurred, it was best to keep Patrick and Audrey in a secure location. Gary's interest was getting a deal for Mike.

As Gary explained it, federal prosecutors in Mike's drug and fraud cases told him that if he informed in a case of this magnitude, his brother would get leniency.

Deputies asked him if he would give them permission to go into Jimmy's room and conduct a search. Gary said sure. Two minutes later, the group was at the front desk asking for a pass key.

Without any hesitation, the night manager turned one over to the deputies.

It was 3:00 a.m. when deputies approached the door of the room where Jimmy and Audrey were asleep. Upon the first knock, there was no answer. They knocked again, even louder this time. Again, no answer.

At this point, deputies used the pass key they got from the front desk and entered the tiny and dark hotel room.

"What do you want?" Jimmy snarled.

"We didn't do anything," Audrey whimpered.

With Gary and Mark now standing just outside the door, the deputies explained that the couple were going to be "detained" in connection with a homicide.

When they searched the dingy motel room, they found watches, a set of apartment keys, and a Russian birth certificate in plain view on the floor.

The deputies at this point had no idea a murder had, in fact, occurred. All they had was the phone call from an attorney and the interviews with Mark and Gary Itaev.

Gary hadn't seen anything, and Mark was either intentionally vague or simply didn't know exactly what version of events was most appropriate.

It was a tricky situation to sort out. Even taking this young couple to the station might not prove anything or yield any more information.

Gary and Mark insisted the cops had to investigate further. Once Audrey and Jimmy were in the back of a patrol car, the patrol deputies reached out to Sheriff's Homicide in Commerce, and detectives headed out to Markzitser's apartment on Sierra Bonita.

Jimmy and Audrey were detained while deputies searched Markzitser's apartment. Although Jimmy said he had locked the bedroom door from the inside when he left, it didn't take long for detectives to discover the body on the bed.

The locked bedroom door had been violently forced open by someone desperate to get inside the tiny bedroom, so much so that the exterior doorknob had been wrenched free. According to one officer, it appeared as if the person inside the bedroom had done everything possible to keep the intruder from getting in but failed.

Whoever did it was desperate to get in and wiped the doorknob clean before leaving, but there were plenty of fingerprints in the bedroom. Mark's were inside the dresser, Kitlas's on top of the dresser, and there were six other prints that couldn't be identified.

Because the Sheriff's Department homicide solve rate hovered below 50 percent, detectives were delighted to have suspects and alleged witnesses handed them so easily. Still, there were interviews to get done.

As the sun burned off the morning fog and a warm afternoon began to take shape, sheriff's detectives Sgt. Ken Clark and Investigator Gabrielle Graves interrogated Mark, but only after Gary, Audrey, and a constantly crying Patrick James Kitlas gave their versions of events.

Rock solid in his accurate explanation of the situation, Gary made it clear that he and Mark were informants for the DEA and were involved in this for the purpose of helping Mike Itaev get released from prison. Mark, however, didn't know that Gary had already provided detectives with such accurate, if damning, information.

The first person arrested for murder was, of course, pregnant and shocked Audrey Lane. This is a common tactic to compel a confession, usually a false one, from the boyfriend to protect the girlfriend. They also took Mark into custody to grill him like a swordfish.

Now it was up to detectives to sort out what had happened in Markzitser's apartment before they arrived.

MAN IN THE BLACK PICKUP

According to court records, Gary Itaev, a registered informant for the Drug Enforcement Agency, testified to his version of the events.

About 1:20 a.m., Gary said he received an urgent call from his nephew Mark, who was also an informant. On the call, Mark sounded tense. He told Gary about the slaying of Sasha Markzitser. A seasoned operative working to shorten his brother's 12-year federal sentence, Gary delivered a calculated response. "Let's call a lawyer."

Court documents showed that Gary and Mark were feeding tips to the DEA and FBI under an agreement to secure leniency for Mike, and Mark pitched this case to Gary as their potential breakthrough.

Gary said that he got into his black pickup and drove to the intersection of Romaine Street and Sierra Bonita Avenue. He said Mark was waiting on the sidewalk. This narrative contradicts Jimmy noticing that black pickup tracking him even before he arrived on Sierra Bonita.

Once inside Gary's truck, Mark described a violent encounter. He said he told Gary he had met Shadow and Audrey that day for the first time and that they were homeless.

Sasha, he explained, after drinking vodka with Mark, had made advances toward Audrey, who allegedly agreed to a sexual encounter.

Mark said that Jimmy, unaware of the arrangement Sasha had with Audrey, killed the man in a violent rage. Mark admitted his fingerprints were in the apartment and that he had used Sasha's phone.

Both Mark and Gary worried about Mark's exposure and at that point agreed to turn Jimmy over to the authorities.

That's when Jimmy showed up.

Gary, fearing Jimmy would flee and leave Mark to take the blame, offered the young man a ride.

They drove back to the 7-Eleven on Santa Monica Boulevard and picked up Audrey. Gary said he told the couple he would take them to a motel.

Gary also recalled that Mark asked Jimmy if he had killed "the guy." According to Gary, Jimmy's demeanor was calm and defiant. He confirmed that he had killed Sasha. Gary said Jimmy went on to boast that he was a hitman who had killed 74 other men.

With everyone in his truck, Gary stepped away to call nan attorney familiar with Mike's case. He wanted to know if turning in a murderer would help his brother.

Court testimony shows that the attorney reached out to a DEA handler, who directed her to the Sheriff's Department. After the call, Gary returned to tell Jimmy and Audrey that he would book a motel room for the night.

By 2:15 a.m., Jimmy and Audrey were settled at the Econo Lodge. Gary and Mark, with their attorney on the line, called the Los Angeles Sheriff's Department. Gary said that during the call, they disclosed their informant status and gave details about Sasha's murder. Deputies said they would be right over.

Meanwhile, Mark and Gary surveilled the Econo Lodge, making sure Jimmy and Audrey didn't sneak out.

Still outside, they urged the officers to approach quietly, without sirens. Around 3:00 a.m., Gary said he met a deputy on Vine Street, finalizing the plan. Deputies entered the Econo Lodge, arresting Jimmy and Audrey.

Gary later told detectives he acted to secure Mike's future, providing names of U.S. Attorneys involved in his brother's case. For him, the night was a strategic play, delivering suspects to authorities in a case he believed could reshape his family's fate.

Now there was a murder to solve. Homicide detectives faced several questions, and they needed answers.

First and foremost, who really killed Aleks Markzitser?

Was it Shadow? The crying kid they had picked up in the motel several hours earlier? Or was it Mark Itaev, the Russian guy who turned in Shadow and Audrey Lane in hopes of getting Meir "Mike" Itaev out of federal custody?

What about the girl? She had played some role in the events that led up to Markzitser's death. Could all of them have acted together?

What did they hope to gain? And why?

AN INFORMANT'S TALE

Interview Room, Sheriff's Bureau, West Hollywood.

Present are Sheriff's Sgt. Ken Clark and his partner Gabrielle Graves. Also present is murder suspect Mark Itaev.

Clark is a veteran homicide detective and by all accounts one of the good guys in a department that can swing either way.

A guy who shaves his head every day, Clark is a man who looks good in a well-pressed suit and also one of the key deputies of the L.A. Sheriff's Department who have earned the "Bulldog" nickname that is applied to the department's homicide cops.

Just two weeks before he caught the Markzitser case, Clark was working a whodunnit involving a well-decomposed body floating in the Pacific Ocean. There was little to go on thanks to how sea water treats a body that has been in its embrace for weeks.

"All we knew was we had a deceased known as John Doe Number Eighty-eight... and his body had been found floating in the Pacific Ocean, seven miles north of Isthmus Harbor, Catalina Island, on May 18, 2006."

He added, "The body was discovered by pleasure boaters sailing from Newport Beach Harbor on a pleasure cruise to Catalina Island. They wisely stayed near the body and put out a mayday with the coordinates. Los Angeles County Sheriff's deputies and paramedics from Catalina Island were dispatched and ultimately recovered the remains."

A key to the body's identity was the fact that the corpse was missing three fingers on his left hand.

"It was in such a state that we really don't know what the gender or the race is," Clark told *Crime Watch Daily*.

Clark and other cops wondered if the decedent had been on a pleasure cruise or a fishing trip and had fallen overboard. But there were no reports of any such incident either in their records or in those maintained by the U.S. Coast Guard.

After an investigation by the Los Angeles County Coroner's Office, detectives had a better idea of what was going on. They had a man who had died as the result of a single gunshot wound to the back of his head.

Now they went to work trying to figure out who it was and who might have done the killing.

When detectives put out a public call for help, almost immediately Clark was contacted by someone who wanted to know if the dead man was missing fingers.

That led Clark to identify the body as that of Steven B. Williams, a 64-year-old resident of Corona del Mar, an Orange County retirement community on the coast between Newport Beach and Laguna. In better days, Williams had been a popular Denver, Colorado AM radio personality who hosted the city's most popular morning show, *Steven B and the Hawk*.

The show featured skits and mildly risqué takes on the day's news at a time when AM radio morning zoos, as they were called then, were stretching the patience of censors across America to compete with Howard Stern and other "shock jocks."

Williams had retired from Denver radio to Southern California in hopes of living a good life with a $2 million inheritance and savings from his days on the air.

In L.A., he hooked up with Harvey Morrow, a self-styled investment guru, who convinced the former disc jockey he had good financial plays that would turn Williams's $2 million into many, many millions more.

Morrow was sinking the money into his own pockets, using some to refurbish a yacht he hoped to take on a world cruise. The rest either went up his nose or rained down on strippers at his favorite L.A. club.

No matter what you might think, $2 million doesn't really have a lot of legs, and it didn't take long before Morrow had run through Williams's inheritance—without Williams's knowledge.

Once the dough disappeared, Williams figured out he was getting scammed. He called for a meeting. Morrow said sure, meet me at the docks, we'll take a ride on my yacht.

Somewhere out on the Pacific between Newport and Catalina, Williams turned his back on his business partner, which is never a good idea when you're arguing over embezzlement. Morrow cranked a round into the back of Williams's head and tossed him overboard.

The case was top of mind when Clark sat down with Itaev as it was his last call out.

Like many of the Bulldogs that make up Sheriff's Homicide, Clark is an imposing guy. If he wasn't a cop, he would probably be a football coach somewhere. The Sheriff's Department always favored big cops for their Homicide Bureau. A lot of them came over from working Robbery or Gangs, both of which take big people to be able to perform the twin tasks of knocking down doors and wrestling with suspects who don't want to serve time in Pelican Bay or San Quentin or even Folsom, for that matter.

That size advantage makes it easier to conduct interviews. Once you've got a suspect cuffed and sitting in the interrogation room, he or she is less likely to be combative if they're facing some football coach/confessor. It was Clark who opened the line of questioning with Itaev.

At this point in a homicide investigation, detectives rely on a checklist of basic steps that should be undertaken or considered so that they will have gathered the best and most accurate information from the witnesses.

The checklist is extensive. First, detectives need to make sure their suspects are unable to revisit the crime scene. Also, their interviews need to be airtight.

"A favorite trick of defense counsel is to distort any custodial interrogation by innuendo, suggesting there was some impropriety on the part of the police in obtaining any statement," author Vernon Gebeth notes in the fifth edition of his 2015 book, *Practical Homicide Investigation: Tactics, Procedures, and Forensic Techniques.*

Many departments employ what's known as the Reid Technique of interrogation. This method breaks down into three parts.

First, you have factual analysis.

The facts of the Markzitser case were still a bit fuzzy.

What was known, courtesy of his eager-to-share uncle Gary Itaev, was that Mark was an informant for the DEA and FBI.

Gary bragged that he and Mark had worked on several cases as informants. The sole motivation for coming forward was to get Meir "Mike" Itaev out of prison.

Someone mentioned that it was Mark's attorney who called the cops. The only other facts the detective knew at the start of the interrogation was that Jimmy and Audrey were in custody, and Sasha was very, very dead.

So, what cops like Clark do is evaluate what the suspect is telling them against what they know to be the truth.

Mark Itaev began his interview with an easily contradicted lie that he had never met Kitlas and Lane until the night of the murder.

Why he thought to establish credibility by blatant dishonesty remains a mystery, but of all the mysteries encountered, this is among those least demanding of an explanation. Stupidity will suffice until a better answer is offered.

The second part of a Reid Technique interview is behavior analysis. There is something about the body language of an innocent person that differs from someone who is guilty.

How someone makes eye contact—or whether they make eye contact at all—is important. How they sit in the chair, adjust to the cuffs, and their willingness to talk or not talk, all play a role in the behavior analysis portion of the interview.

At this juncture of an interview, an investigator will ask their suspect background questions. This helps them gather personal information and evaluate a baseline normal verbal and nonverbal behavior.

There is an objective standard that can be established, and it allows the detective to decide if a suspect is telling the truth or not. Here a detective is also gathering insight into the interview subject and hopefully developing a rapport with the suspect. It gives the good detective a strategy roadmap for dealing with the person being interrogated.

At some point, the detective will switch to what are known as "behavior provoking questions." This series of questions and answers will give the investigator a way to begin separating truth from fiction.

At this point, the third step of a Reid interrogation usually gets underway. And it was here that Clark began with Mark.

Jimmy remembered how the fluorescent lights of the West Hollywood Station interrogation room buzzed faintly overhead. He recalled the lights casting a sterile glow over a worn stainless steel table.

Mark Itaev sat in the same spot. It was 3:22 a.m. on June 8, 2004. Jimmy said Mark probably felt some of the same internal distress he did. His mouth was dry, his nerves frayed from the relentless back-and-forth.

Mark had asked for water earlier. He was still waiting on it when Clark leaned forward, his voice measured but unyielding.

"Let's go over this again, Mark. When you were at the 7-Eleven and saw the police officers, why didn't you tell them what you'd seen earlier?"

Mark shifted in his chair, his fingers twitching against the tabletop. "It all happened so fast," he said, his voice low, halting. "I saw the sheriff's car pulling up, and then my uncle showed up in the driveway from Santa Monica. It was, like, a minute. I didn't have time to think. He just… he told me to get in the car."

"Your uncle told you to get in the car?" Clark's eyebrow arched, his pen hovering over his notepad.

"Yeah." Mark nodded.

Clark's questions turned to Jimmy, the man whose name hung heavy in the air. "You said Jimmy told you he moved the body. Tell me about that again."

Mark haltingly responded. "He said he moved it from the floor… put it on the bed, or maybe a chair. I'm not sure exactly what he said."

The detective's tone changed. "Mark, I need you to listen carefully before you answer. Did you help Patrick move that body?"

"No, sir," Mark said.

"Did you help tie him up?"

"No, sir."

"Did you touch Aleks at any point that evening, before he was murdered?"

Mark hesitated. "I shook his hand," he said finally, the words careful, deliberate. "That's it."

Clark continued to press. "That's the only contact you had with Aleks?"

"Yes."

The interrogation pressed on, each question peeling back another layer of the night in question. Clark asked whose idea it had been to introduce Aleks to Jimmy and Audrey. Jimmy, Mark answered, his voice steadier now, though his palms were slick with sweat.

"When you and your uncle decided to put them in a hotel room," Clark continued, "did you know then that Aleks was dead?"

"No," Mark said, shaking his head. "I only found out when we went to the police, after everything at the apartment."

But Clark wanted to know if there had been any confession by Jimmy. "Did you have a conversation with Patrick at any time in the presence of anyone, your uncle or Audrey, where Patrick admitted that he had murdered Aleks?"

Mark nodded slowly. "Yes."

"Was that before you went to the police or after you went to the police?"

"That was before we went to the police," Mark said, doubling down on an answer that conflicted with his previous response. "That was before we went to the police."

The detective's questions grew more pointed, his patience thinning.

"When you were talking to Patrick and Audrey at the hotel room, did you know that Aleks was dead?"

"No."

The detective asked the same question in a different way, adding Gary into the mix.

"When you and your uncle decided to rent that hotel room, did you know that Aleks was dead?"

Mark began to equivocate. "I only knew that Aleks was dead by Patrick's words."

Clark circled back again. "When you went—when you rented the hotel room for Patrick and Audrey, or your uncle rented that hotel room for Patrick and Audrey, did you know that Aleks was dead?"

Mark began to get fearful.

"No. God—in my eyes, I did not see him dead," he told Clark.

Knowing that Gary had laid out a simple and likely truthful timeline of events, Clark wanted to see how much of Mark's statement would align with his uncle's version of events. If it was aligned, that would indicate Mark was telling the truth. If it varied, it would be because Mark was lying. But where were the lies and where was the truth? Clark would continue to probe Mark's memory.

"Did you ever tell your uncle before he came to the scene to pick you up that Aleks was dead?"

Mark was doing everything he could to throw Jimmy under the bus.

"I told him that [Jimmy], uh, said that he killed him. I never seen him dead in my eyes."

Again, Clark circled back to moments after the murder and putting Audrey and Jimmy into a room at the Econo Lodge. "Did you tell your uncle that Aleks was dead?"

Mark was getting more agitated. "I told him that I think that Patrick killed Aleks."

Clark didn't have the answer he was looking for. Mark was being evasive. He asked again.

The question still was the same. "Did you tell your uncle before he came to pick you up that Aleks was dead?"

Now Mark was firm. "No, I did not."

Clark zeroed in on Gary and Mark's deal with the DEA.

"Did you talk to your uncle about what you would do if Aleks was dead?"

Mark remained evasive.

Clark was getting exasperated.

"Do you understand my question?" the detective asked. "Did you talk with your uncle about what you would do, and your uncle would do, if Aleks was dead?"

Mark began a half answer, then stopped, claiming he continued to misunderstand. What he did say was more like a word salad.

"We would create, as far as contacting the lawyer—I mean, I don't, I don't understand the question, sir."

Clark went back to the same territory.

"The question is very simple. Listen to my question: Did you talk with—at—with your uncle about what you and he would do if Aleks was dead?"

Defeated, Mark finally answered. "Yes."

Clark put a pin in it.

"So you knew Aleks was dead when you talked to your uncle?"

Mark backtracked.

"No. If... well, you asked me if he was dead."

"So you knew Aleks was dead when you called your uncle?"

Mark said he only knew Sasha was dead because someone told him. "I didn't physically see him dead."

Clark reverted to the timeline as he understood it from what Gary, Audrey, and Mark had already laid out. It was here that the detective deployed a tactic right out of the Reid Technique interrogation playbook: overcoming the objection.

It's a term of art usually used in sales.

Say you're buying a new car and you get to the point where you realize the monthly payments are too high or you can't afford insurance, or you don't like the color of the car you're thinking of buying.

Typically, you will raise an objection. It is the salesperson's goal to isolate your objection and overcome it. With detective work, the objection is isolated and then thrown in the suspect's face as proof a lie has been uttered.

Here's what Reid says about overcoming objections: "When attempts at denial fail, a guilty suspect often makes objections to support a claim of innocence (e.g., I would never do that because I love my job). The investigator should generally accept these objections as if they were truthful, rather than arguing with the suspect, and use the objections to further develop the theme."

"You just told me that Audrey came to you and told you that he killed Aleks. You told me you went down to the apartment, and you saw him tied up. *After* Audrey told you he was killed. You told me you saw him snap his neck. You told me that [Jimmy] told you at some point he had taken the body and put it on the bed. You told me that during this time that [Jimmy] was in the room taking personal items belonging to Aleks. And that you went into that very same bedroom and closed the drawers as he ransacked and took the items out of those drawers. Is that true?"

Mark was trapped, and he protested. "I didn't say that! You're confusing me."

Clark continued to press.

"And then you went in, and you went and got your dog, and you left. Is that true?"

Mark jumped at the opportunity to answer. "That's right."

Now that Clark had Mark pinned down to a specific timeline, the veteran detective dug in for more.

"And then you stood at the corner, and you waited at the 7-Eleven until at some point—according to you—what you just told me, [Jimmy] went back to that house and took Aleks and put him on that bed. Is that not what you told me?"

Mark fumbled for an answer.

Clark continued.

"Now, while you waited at the corner at the 7-Eleven, you decided at that point that you were gonna call your uncle. Is that correct?"

Mark began to catch on to the game of cat and mouse that had him trapped. He was hesitant to answer. It was almost as if he was waiting to see where the detective was going, as if he could out-maneuver the interrogation.

And Clark, who had practiced his profession against some of the world's best liars, continued to go over the timeline.

"When did you decide to call your uncle?"

"I just called my uncle as we were walking on Curson... going towards the 7-Eleven."

Clark tightened his questioning.

"Okay, so your—your testimony to me is that you called your uncle at what time?"

Mark said he didn't know or remember.

Clark wanted something.

"What did you say to your uncle, and how long did the conversation last?"

Mark continued to struggle, hoping to tease out the direction of the questions.

Again, Clark continued to push. "Tell me exactly what you said to your uncle?"

Mark had to say something, and he offered up a response.

"I told my uncle listen, I think that, uh—uh, this guy killed somebody, and I need you to please come and pick me up."

Clark's main thrust in questioning continued to be, what did Mark know and when did he know it?

"So, at that time, you believed Aleks was dead. It doesn't matter whether you think or not. You said dead."

Mark began to stutter and whine. "'Cause that's what they told me, Patrick and—and—and—"

The veteran detective cut off his suspect and hinted that he knew Mark was trying to shift blame and responsibility by coloring his story to fit what he thought the detective knew.

"So, are you playing mind games here or what?"

Mark stammered. He backtracked. He couldn't say when he called his uncle or if he told his uncle that Sasha was dead.

Clark finally had enough.

"This is a very serious case. Okay? You're going to be booked for murder."

Now Mark was scared. "Why?"

Clark turned cold. "Is there anything else you wanna add?"

Mark continued to stammer. Now he was sweating. "Actually, I w-what should I, I did not kill this—this person."

Clark responded, "That's fine. I'll put that in my report."

Mark continued to insist. Now he was whimpering.

"I did not kill this person, and I wasn't a part of this, sir. I reported it to the police."

"Yes, you did," Clark answered in a way that wasn't clear if he was responding to the first part of the statement or the second. "I don't believe you."

Mark got more desperate. "What? Why?"

Then the detective dropped a bomb.

"Your uncle said something completely different than what you're telling me."

Mark tried to elicit more. "How could my uncle say something completely different?"

"I'm not gonna tell you what he told me. It's up to you to find out through your attorney what your uncle told us. As far as I'm concerned, I'm gonna end this conversation. Is there anything else you wanna add? I don't have time to talk to you anymore."

Mark exhaled and sighed. "Only I didn't do anything. I did not have nothing to do with this."

Clark took a different tact and pressed for more.

"Okay. Is that the statement you want—you want me to put on the report? Would you like for me to add the fact that you and your uncle decided to call an attorney and use this to get your uncle off the criminal case that he had with the DEA? And you are a DEA informant, is that correct?"

Mark replied simply, "Yeah, we're working for the—with the DEA."

Clark wanted to understand the motivation behind Mark and Gary's efforts to put Jimmy and Audrey in trouble for Sasha's murder. "Okay. You say, 'We're working for the DEA.' Are you working on behalf of getting somebody off of a criminal case that they have?"

Mark's mood momentarily brightened.

Clark shot him back down.

"Okay. Are you aware that it is—that this case has no bearing in that? Are you aware... Are you aware that I am not giving you nor will I authorize any leniency towards you in the murder of Aleks that was committed here in the West Hollywood Station's area? I've offered you no leniency. I will not offer any leniency. At this point, I'm gonna stop talking to you because I've pretty much said what I had to say."

Clark turned off his tape recorder. His interview with Mark had taken all of 12 minutes.

Elsewhere in the station, Jimmy just wanted to sleep.

THE OTHER SUSPECT

In a separate interrogation room, Jimmy Kitlas alternated between weeping and dozing off. Occasionally, Clark or another detective would come in and wake him up. He was getting a modern version of the third degree via sleep deprivation.

All he wanted was some shuteye. The events of the night had worn him out—physically and emotionally.

When the detectives came in, they would ask questions. He would be evasive and tear up. Finally, Jimmy waived his Miranda rights and began to talk.

Geberth's investigative manual notes that it is critically important to evaluate a suspect's demeanor and mental capacity.

Jimmy didn't want them to charge Audrey with murder or accessory and figured the best thing to do was to admit his role and take responsibility.

After initially claiming that he only took items from Sasha's apartment at Mark's instruction, Jimmy ultimately took responsibility for all of it—even the killing. That was because he knew how serious Clark was, and Jimmy believed that if he didn't take the fall, they were going to charge Audrey with murder. He was correct.

Geberth's manual also urges detectives to gauge their suspect's opinion of the victim.

They asked Jimmy if he was mad that Sasha wanted to sleep with Audrey. He said he didn't know that and didn't even remember being angry at any time during the fatal attack.

With Jimmy's confession, Mark's evasion, and Audrey's promise to testify for the prosecution, Clark's work was quickly done. He would go on to his next case, while Mark and Jimmy awaited trial.

The Los Angeles County District Attorney's Office charged Jimmy and Mark with murder, robbery, and burglary but cut a deal with Audrey Lane: if she testified against her boyfriend, she wouldn't be prosecuted, and she could keep her baby.

Kids like her are terrified of cops and courts and anything that comes from the monolith of power—the government.

If you're not poor, if you're not living on the street, you don't know the non-stop fear of police, the disdain with which you're looked upon, the constant paranoia that anyone or everyone will rip you off, rob you, take advantage of you, and get away with it because you're poor and homeless and they're not, or they have authority and you don't.

The disadvantaged street youth, even those of legal age, are at a double disadvantage due to the criminalization of poverty.

In the musical *Fiddler on the Roof*, Tevya, a poor milkman, says, "It is no crime to be poor, but it is no great honor either." In America, Tevya is wrong. It is a crime to be poor, and it is still no great honor.

"It has become a crime to be poor. If you are poor enough to be homeless, you are really fucked," Kelley Leigh said. "If you are a school kid, misbehavior that used to get you sent to the principal's office will now get you hauled off to juvenile court."

Tragically true, and even more so in the 21st century.

For instance, in February 2020, a special needs six-year-old girl with ADHD and mood disorder was arrested by police, handcuffed in the classroom, and taken away begging for help. The reason for her arrest? She had thrown a tantrum earlier in the day at her Orlando, Florida elementary school.

And get this: if you're a woman getting the crap beat out of you by an abusive husband or boyfriend, you can be evicted for calling the police too many times. True. If the city in which you live has "nuisance property ordinances," frequent visits by police are cause for eviction even if the police are coming there to save you.

If you're fortunate enough to live in a home or apartment with a non-abusive significant other, these traps set to snare the poor and people of color are probably hard to believe.

"It doesn't matter that it is against the law for the cops to steal your stuff," commented a former homeless woman from the streets of Los Angeles. "And if you tell the cops that you know that, they get real pissed off and retaliate against you. They treat you like dirt. They threw away my thyroid meds and my anti-depressants."

"The pattern," wrote author and activist Barbara Ehrenreich in an op-ed piece in *The New York Times*, "is to curtail financing for services that might help the poor while ramping up law enforcement: starve school and public transportation budgets, then make truancy illegal. Shut down public housing, then make it a crime to be homeless."

Now, picture a mentally challenged, child-like young adult living on the street in Hollywood with an equally homeless pregnant girlfriend, being befriended by a low-level criminal specializing in identity theft and exploitation of others for his own ends.

Mark Itaev was working for the Pasadena PD as an informant at the same time he was forging checks. Pasadena has a long history with informants. Some of that interaction has resulted in meaningful arrests, but much of the interaction worked as a shortcut to real police work.

For example, during the investigation of 1993's Halloween murders—in which three young trick-or-treaters were shot and killed by Blood gang members who mistook them for a rival gang—Pasadena police used jailhouse informants to develop leads in the case.

One of the informants, testifying in court, explained that he had been arrested on a bogus charge of using a car without the owner's permission.

"I spoke to a Hispanic officer who said they were going to give me a charge of joyriding," recalled the informant, who had a rap sheet that included battery, forgery, and unlawful restraint. "But they told me that if I gave them information about what I knew about the Halloween shooting, I would get out of my case."

When the cops needed his testimony, they put the informant up in a fancy hotel and let him charge up all the room service he needed to keep him happy.

The Pasadena PD wasn't the only organization working with Mark Itaev. According to court documents, he was regularly working with the DEA as well.

The agreement both sides worked out was simple. Helpful information provided by Itaev was ranked on a sliding scale.

Higher-ranking instances of cooperation would conceivably lower his uncle's (Mike Itaev's) time on the fraud case he had caught with Daniel Patterson and an unrelated drug case.

A large part of Jimmy's case focused on Mark's role as an associate of the Russian Mafia but made no mention of him being an informant.

Kitlas's lawyers described Itaev's associates and family members as members of a criminal gang that profited from extortion, drug dealing, financial crimes, and prostitution.

The Kitlas lawyers also knew Itaev had been in trouble earlier in 2004, when he was arrested at the Commerce Casino.

"Every time I saw Jimmy with Mark," says Kelley Leigh, "it gave me the creeps. Hell, Itaev and I were selling pot and coke out of the same motel, and that's when he was already a sworn-in agent and confidential informant. If he didn't have his sights set on exploiting somebody else, he could have focused on screwing with my life."

Jimmy didn't stand a chance on the streets, just like he hadn't stood a chance in school. And he didn't stand a chance in court.

There are those who mistakenly think, "If they could just get these kids in school, everything would be okay."

Wrong.

Street kids almost always struggle to integrate into regular school programs because of the attendance requirements. They also become frustrated because the topics taught are irrelevant to their lives.

Street kids usually experience discrimination in class, and because they have limited family support, if any, they often fail to complete homework on time. Their manner of dress and personal presentation may not be appropriate for school.

"The fact is," says educator Britt Elin, "they can't simply enroll in formal education and benefit from it. The highest number of school dropouts are street children. Street kids, regardless of age, need specialized and often individualized approaches that directly address the real-life issues they face every day. It is the same with high school-age students who come from other cultures, even other cultures within the USA. They are fifteen to sixteen years old, married with children, and feel completely out of place in high school teenage prom date culture. To them, it is useless nonsense."

Attempts to rescue street kids aren't viewed favorably by those supposedly being rescued. Much as victims of human trafficking will run away from their safe suburban foster home to go back to sex work on the streets of their own volition, people gravitate toward that with which they're familiar and comfortable.

"The funny thing," says Kelley, "was that Jimmy Kitlas came from a comfortable lifestyle. His grandparents aren't poor, nor was he mistreated by them. He needed professional care and individual therapy. Instead, he got abuse and a bus ticket. To hope for justice as the outcome of that situation is to be overly optimistic."

CELEBRITY JUSTICE

Not long after they were arrested, Jimmy and Mark had their case assigned to a courtroom in the Beverly Hills Courthouse.

The mid-century modern courthouse is within walking distance of the Beverly Hills City Hall and police station made famous in movies like *Beverly Hills Cop.*

The courthouse had other reasons to be famous. Any time a movie star got married, divorced, pulled over for drunk driving, caught smoking weed, hanging out in the men's room at a nearby public park, or murdered, there was a good chance their case would end up in the Beverly Hills courthouse, splashed on the front page of every supermarket tabloid, or featured on such TV shows as *E! True Hollywood Stories.*

The Kitlas/Itaev case had none of that. What it did have was celebrity judge Elden S. Fox.

Assigned to the Beverly Hills courthouse for 27 years, Judge Fox was no stranger to celebrities.

He had presided over cases ranging from rocker Tommy Lee's alleged abuse of his ex-wife, actress Pamela Anderson, to *Beverly Hills 90210* star Shannon Doherty's nightclub brawling case and actress Winona Ryder's infamous shoplifting trial.

Before Fox became a judge, he gained notoriety as the prosecutor who helped convict Zsa Zsa Gabor in 1989 of slapping a police officer, driving without a license, and possessing a flask of Jack Daniels on the front seat of her car, the smell of booze emanating from her breath.

In his 70-minute closing arguments, Fox told jurors that the aging Hungarian actress and socialite, the first influencer—famous for merely being famous—viewed the courtroom as a stage where "she came to entertain you."

Gabor disrupted her 13-day trial that made international headlines, often dramatically running out of the courtroom in tears.

A 13-day trial is a luxury in L.A. County, where in 1989, prosecutors were dealing with crack cocaine cases, murder, attempted murder, prostitution, check fraud, assaults, and robbery.

Even though the case was a joke, Fox blamed the media for prolonging the punchline.

"She craves the media attention in this case, it is clear," Fox told the jury. "The thing that outrages me most is she used and abused two weeks of this process for her own aggrandizement. The defendant doesn't know the meaning of truth… Her perception of truth differs from facts in the case."

When Zsa Zsa broke down in tears and fled the courtroom for the fourth time in two weeks, she complained that Fox was impolite and unfair.

She said Fox had a "Napoleon complex," while he called the highly publicized case "the greatest thing to happen to that post-menopausal lady's career."

Fox found himself channeling Zsa Zsa (without the tears) in 1995 when he and his wife, Janet Fox, a senior county prosecutor, were sued by the DJ they hired for their daughter's bat mitzvah after the Foxes refused to pay him $1,692—the outstanding amount they owed him for services. The case gave a glimpse of the judge's temperament.

During the litigation, Fox asked for a change of venue, filed a legal brief that included 18 exhibits, and demanded to bring a stenographer to court, a service not provided for a small claims case. He even walked out of court for dramatic effect. It turns out one can learn things from menopausal stars after all.

It didn't work. The court commissioner entered a default judgment against the Foxes, which they appealed, complaining that the commissioner had chosen "to 'flex his muscle' and punish the defendants."

The case dragged on for five months. A superior court judge overturned the judgment and ordered the two sides to split the difference.

The judge and Janet were convinced they were vindicated by the Superior Court's decision.

"Are we expected, that when someone breaches a contract, we have to grin and bear it and pay the amount?" Janet Fox remarked to *The Los Angeles Times*.

Because of the raw emotions displayed at trial, the commissioner said the case didn't reflect well on the system. Fox eventually conceded that he shouldn't have walked out of the courtroom.

By 2002, Fox was no longer a prosecutor. Instead, he was the judge, getting his first taste of celebrity justice from the bench presiding over actress Winona Ryder's shoplifting trial.

Unlike Gabor, Ryder's crime was caught on video tape. Cameras in the high-end Sacks Fifth Avenue in Beverly Hills caught the actress—at the height of her fame—grabbing stuff off the racks, cutting off the tags in dressing rooms, and boosting high-end clothes like a pro.

But even pros get caught. Ryder was stopped by store security on her way out with an arm load of stuff that would be out of style by summer.

A jury convicted Ryder of stealing more than $5,500 worth of merchandise a year later.

Fox spared Ryder any jail time, aside from the time she spent behind bars while she was being booked. He ordered her to pay $10,000 in fines and restitution and perform 480 hours of community service that would be served at City of Hope, a cancer hospital near Los Angeles. Because she had no prior convictions, prosecutors only asked for probation.

"It is not my intention to make an example of you," Fox told Ryder. But he said she had disappointed many people, and she would have to confront certain issues that led to her behavior, like opiate addiction. Her arrest revealed that Ryder had a pharmacy in her purse that included Oxys, Percocets, Valium, morphine, codeine, and liquid Demerol of the sort used only by experienced junkies, i.e., the kind who tie off and shoot up in a basement.

A few years later, Judge Fox was presiding over the trial of Itaev and Kitlas.

Among the first items to come out in Fox's court was the acknowledgement that Mark Itaev wasn't the man he seemed to be.

Jimmy said he hit an all-time low when he was unceremoniously, if not accidentally, was informed via court documents that Mark Itaev was an official agent of law enforcement.

Mark inviting him into the black pickup the night of the murder would qualify as a mildly amusing pleasant surprise compared to the sudden revelation that the fellow who represented himself as the manifestation of sophisticated criminality with an identity theft specialty was, in fact, a confidential informant working for not only the local police but also the federal government. It was like dumping anger-activated hot coals on Kitlas's resentment center.

The child-like gentleman who avoided physical fights suddenly wanted to commit a wide variety of fantasized acts of fatal illegality upon his former mentor as retaliation for what was now perceived as blatant and obvious intentional deception and manipulation.

"No shit," Jimmy said. "When I found out he was an informant I was furious, outraged, and just wished I could get some sort of explanation out of him. It was disappointing and disheartening to realize this jerk had played me for a sucker."

If there was ever a case custom-crafted for an entrapment defense, this one was it: A government agent, by means of influence, manipulation, and intimidation induced Jimmy Kitlas to engage in crimes, entrapping him in violation of his Fifth, Eighth, and Fourteenth Amendment rights of the United States Constitution and Article 1 Section 7 of the California State Constitution.

"After being arrested, and during proceedings in court," says Kitlas, "I felt I was being professionally set up to be convicted of a crime which I was talked into committing by an agent of law enforcement to benefit his uncle.

"During my trial, and prior to the trial itself, I repeatedly asked my lead counsel to put on an entrapment defense as I was set up, and that's the defense I wished to be presented to my jury. Counsel refused all my requests, and the same requests made by my grandparents and by another lawyer, who was fired for requesting the entrapment defense."

"Did you hear that?" Kelley later asked. "I mean, what the fuck? That's insane. Someone was fired for advocating for the most obvious defense."

It wasn't just that. Prosecutor Marcia Beth Daniel was accused of rigging jury selection so that anyone who had a distrust of law enforcement wasn't selected to the panel.

Someone was fired, and not by Kitlas nor his grandparents. In fact, both grandparents begged the lead counsel to hear their consistent pleas to honor their grandson's request.

"During court proceedings," Kitlas's grandmother said, "lead counsel enlisted the services of [another attorney]. As matters developed, and facts of the case revealed themselves, [the other attorney] also suggested that lead counsel take the case in another direction and raise the entrapment defense as Patrick's primary defense."

It is important to understand that once the entrapment defense is properly raised, the government must prove that the defendant—Patrick James Kitlas—wasn't entrapped. Considering the seemingly overwhelming and obvious evidence of entrapment at every stage of the crime, the lead trial counsel shouldn't have claimed that not raising the entrapment defense was strategic, especially considering that Kitlas repeatedly requested it, as did the advisor on the case who was fired for making the suggestion.

"I spoke to [the other attorney] several times," Kitlas's grandfather said later, "and she clearly stated that she believed that the reason she was fired was because she continually voiced her firm belief that the entrapment defense should be raised as our grandson's primary defense."

"I'm no legal expert," Kelley Leigh said, "but I have looked it up and I can say with assurance that the attorney had absolutely no authority to continually reject requests to use entrapment, especially when the kid was set up."

"If I am subpoenaed to testify as to why I was fired," the other attorney said to Jimmy's grandparents, who were watching the trial unfold from the sidelines, "I will state under oath that the reason I was fired was because I kept advocating for the use of the entrapment defense."

"Why wouldn't Kitlas's attorney use the most powerful defense available, especially when the defendant's family and their hired advisor literally begged her to do it?" Kelley asked. "It sure as hell wasn't a strategic legal decision in her client's best interest."

CALIFORNIA

An entrapment defense for Jimmy would have been perfectly viable under California law.

Criminal defendants in California have a constitutional right to assert a defense to the charges against them. In some cases, they can claim a defense of entrapment. This involves proving that law enforcement induced them to commit a crime. Because Mark and Gary claimed they were working on behalf of law enforcement, Jimmy and him family could have expected the rules to apply.

Here is a detailed explanation of what is and isn't entrapment in California.

Examples of Entrapment in California

These are some examples of conduct by a law enforcement officer or agent that could amount to entrapment in California:

- Encouraging a person to engage in criminal conduct as a way of proving themself to the officer or agent: "To prove I can trust you, you have to do this shooting."

- Using excessive flattery designed to overcome someone's doubts about committing a crime: "Do this job with me, and you'll see that this is what you were born to do."

- Threatening a person or that person's loved ones with harm if a person does not commit a crime: "Something bad will happen to your family if you don't go in with me on doing this drug crime."

- Appealing to friendship or sympathy to convince someone to break the law: "I'm only asking you to do this crime with me because I have no one else to turn to."

- Guaranteeing that the act isn't a crime: "What I'm proposing we do is a hundred percent legit. Nobody will get hurt, and I promise you won't get in any trouble."

- Offering an extraordinary benefit in exchange for the person taking a relatively small action: "All you need to do is sit there in the car for ten minutes while I do my thing, and I'll pay you $1,000,000."

In contrast to the examples above, it isn't entrapment if the officer or agent did nothing more than allow the defendant to commit the crime or simply tried to gain confidence through reasonable and restrained words or actions. For example, it isn't entrapment for an undercover agent to help arrange a drug transaction or to agree to play a role in a kidnapping.

Entrapment is a defense. It is up to the criminal defendant's lawyer to raise and prove it in court by a preponderance of evidence, demonstrating that it is more likely than not that the defendant was entrapped. This is a lower standard than the burden of proof the prosecutor must meet to convict them of a crime.

Criminal defense lawyers make a case for entrapment by presenting evidence and arguments focused primarily on the law enforcement officer's or agent's conduct.

They often also seek to paint a clear picture of the context in which that conduct took place to help the jury evaluate what a normally law-abiding person in the criminal defendant's shoes would have done in the same situation.

If proven, entrapment entitles you to acquittal on the charged crime.

With the entrapment defense so obvious, why was the jury never told that Mark and Gary were agents of law enforcement working this scenario to get Meir "Mike" Itaev out of prison?

A Los Angeles County prosecutor put it bluntly. "The DEA, a federal government agency, insisted that Mark Itaev's status as a confidential informant not be revealed because he was an important asset. So, both the prosecution and defense agreed to have that information suppressed as a favor to the DEA, FBI, or both."

Of course, Kitlas was never told about the prosecution and defense having agreed on the suppression of the most important element of this tragic story.

At trial, Mark testified against Jimmy, even going so far as to relate a fictional narrative of him being present when, according to Mark, Jimmy violently twisted Sasha's head until the poor man's neck, made a sickening sound.

"I was stunned to hear him say that. He wasn't even there when I threw Aleks to the floor. I never twisted the man's neck. Aleks was very drunk and out of it, but he was alive and breathing when we left, and I locked the bedroom door behind me."

Most disturbing is that both the prosecution and the defense had access to a coroner's report that showed no indication of damage to Sasha's neck whatsoever.

When Sasha was assuredly dead, the testimony timeline indicates Mark called his attorney from the dead man's telephone, reported the murder, and yanked out the phone line before he returned, agitated and breathless, to the convenience store.

Despite the arresting homicide detective being aware of the Itaevs' status as confidential informants trying to help Mike get released, he was never called to testify. Nor was there any mention of the nature of the crime scene or Gary's admission to both the arriving officers and Detective Clark that he and Mark were working for law enforcement to benefit Meir "Mike" Itaev.

The key and important fact in the entire case was never revealed to the jury. The prosecution knew the truth. The defense knew the truth, and even the judge knew the truth.

"Without that information," noted Fred Wolfson, "it was impossible for Kitlas to have a fair trial. Oh, sure, they portrayed Mark as a bad man, a common criminal with bad family connections, but never, ever was the jury told the truth: every action on the night Aleks died was dictated and directed by an agent of law enforcement."

"It is my opinion," said Kelley Leigh, "that the defense counsel threw the kid under the bus. And speaking of kids, you know about Audrey, right? She believed that if she didn't testify against the father of her child, the baby would be taken from her. Remember, she was the first and, at the time, the only person charged with murder! Yes, Audrey! Don't forget that. There were going to be three trials, Audrey's being the third if they couldn't coerce Kitlas to confess and compel little traumatized Audrey to testify against him at trial."

Chivalry isn't dead; chivalry is deadly. They counted on Kitlas having a sacrificial heart of gold—he took the blame to save Audrey.

The jury in Kitlas's trial had enough reasonable doubt to find him not guilty of murder, but guilty of burglary. The jury was instructed, however, that if they found him guilty of the lesser charges of burglary and theft, they had to also find him guilty of murder. In truth, the jury had no reason to undertake such an absurd obligation.

Patrick James Kitlas, the childlike, non-violent kid, was sentenced to life in prison with the possibility of parole.

EPILOGUE

The second jury acquitted Mark Itaev of killing Aleks "Sasha" Markzitser but convicted him on charges related to his identity theft enterprises. Itaev was sentenced to a six-year, eight-month term.

The plan to get Mike out of prison worked perfectly.

"What does Meir 'Mike' Itaev do once he is free?" Kelley Leigh says. "He becomes a professional poker player, creates a corporation dedicated to energy reclamation or something, and then becomes a highly praised philanthropist for the benefit of disadvantaged youth by founding the Rainbow Children's Academy in Inglewood, California—a daycare for children with special needs, including autism spectrum disorder. Field trips, enrichment activities in gymnastics and karate, summer camp, music lessons, and language studies were also offered."

Press releases proclaimed the reputation and image of Meir Itaev somewhat at odds with his actual resume:

> *Michael "Meir" Itaev continues to be well-known around the world for being a very successful businessman. Today, Itaev is the owner of West Coast Commodity and Technology, which is a company that he founded years ago. This organization is continuing to develop technologies and processes that are helping to improve the*

environment and living conditions all over the world.

"Renewables are important not just for the now, but also the future," Meir Itaev argues on a website for his business. "Through gasification, we can convert biomass and some other substances into carbon monoxide, hydrogen, and carbon dioxide. This creates synthesis gas which can be used as a fuel source."

According to a 2020 press release, Meir Itaev is working on several gasification projects, including a project in Mexico City, which will turn biomass destined for landfills into a useful renewable energy resource.

"I love the environment, and that's a big driver for gasification. People are important too, however. Through gasification, I aim to improve air quality in places like Mexico City," Meir Itaev says. "This could save lives by reducing cancer rates and addressing other issues."

No gasification program with Mexico was ever undertaken by Itaev's corporation. By 2022, the corporation was deemed inactive by the California Secretary of State.

Michael Itaev continued as a founder, donor, and contributor to the Rainbow Children's Academy for many years and, as one press release proclaimed:

Through this organization, he can ensure that kids all over the South Bay region of Los Angeles are cared for and receive the resources they need to live a happy and healthy life.

"I must admire Meir for his rock-solid support of Rainbow Children's Academy in Inglewood, California," said Kelley Leigh. "I would hope that a significant portion of his motivation is that the reason he is a free man and able to help kids is because of a kind, selfless kid named Patrick James Kitlas. I firmly believe Jimmy went to prison as the direct result of manipulation and coercion by an agent of law enforcement—a confidential informant and convicted felon who is also Meir's nephew, Mark Itaev."

Sadly, Rainbow Children's Academy of Inglewood, California, no longer exists. It filed for bankruptcy in 2019.

After several attempts, Jimmy Kitlas finally appeared before the California Board of Parole Hearings in 2024.

His remorse over the death of Aleks was, and is, 100% sincere. He sets aside time every day to remember the man who died that night. Over time, Kitlas took upon himself the full weight of guilt for Aleks's death.

"I had to deal with what was real: I was found guilty of murder. Mark Itaev was found not guilty. Period."

Appearing before the Board of Parole Hearings, Kitlas said, "I was lashing out at this other human being because I felt he stood in my way of the approval that I felt that I desired from Mr. [Itaev]."

Successfully meeting expectations and requirements, Patrick James Kitlas was released from prison a much different man than when he went in as a traumatized, railroaded, deceived, discarded, and exploited teenager with a history of instability, impulsivity, unresolved issues of emotional and sexual abuse, insufficient empathetic counseling, and an overabundance of contraindicated medications.

"In the almost twenty years I spent in prison, I took control of my ADHD to the best of my ability without the bizarre combination of medications I was put on as a teenager. I still deal with it daily, but I have changed a great deal."

It turns out that Kitlas is exceptionally bright and remarkably gifted. He speaks several languages fluently—Russian, Spanish, German, Finnish, Lakota, and

Kumeyaay—plus he's conversational in Urdu and Hindi, and he can learn any language or dialect quickly with remarkable ease.

He also has mastered all crafts associated with the construction field, and more importantly, he has built a firm and unshakeable reputation for honesty and integrity. Strongly connected to his Native American heritage, he left prison with a dedicated support group awaiting him.

Once released from prison, Kitlas established paternal bonds with the estranged daughter of Audrey Lane.

"I hadn't seen Audrey since they sent me away, and for a while I wondered if I really were the father of her child and if I would ever have a relationship with my daughter. We didn't connect in person until I was free. My daughter is twenty years old, has survived a traumatic childhood and even more traumatic young adulthood, and we have established an excellent father/daughter relationship."

Happily married and gainfully employed, the kid once known as Shadow is now a fully grown responsible adult of many admirable talents, qualities, and attributes. He still thinks of Aleksandre Markzitser every day and holds no revenge fantasies or long-term resentments regarding Mark Itaev.

"Mark's life is Mark's life. My life is my life. He did what his best thinking told him to do to help his uncle. Sadly, Aleks died so someone could go free. I did twenty years in prison so someone could go free. They say if you save one life, it is as if you saved all mankind. Because of that excellent program for kids, Meir may have been a blessing to more people's lives than we can imagine. I certainly have nothing at all against Meir Itaev. In fact, I would like to meet the man and let him know I appreciate what he did for the community when he got out of prison. I hope that I am also a blessing to my community now that I am out of prison."

Mark Itaev served his time and served time again following his convictions in the case involving his loving wife, Yelena.

Most recently, Mark seems to have remained crime- and conviction-free, living as a law-abiding citizen with his wife and kids.

Whether or not Mark was still acting as a confidential informant for the DEA and FBI while serving his prison sentences is unknown. DEA officials didn't respond to requests for information about the informants or this case.

Everyone involved in this story is aware of one striking truth: Patrick James Kitlas probably didn't receive a fair trial, as the most important facts of the case were withheld from the jury.

"The trial was a complete travesty of justice," investigator Fred Wolfson said. "I don't know how the prosecutor could sleep at night, or the defense either. The most important fact of the case was never mentioned. Had the jury known the truth, that kid would never have gone to prison. In fact, had the defense pursued the entrapment defense, I believe the case would have been dropped rather than reveal the identity of the confidential informant if the DEA was that dedicated to keeping his identity a secret."

Even the members of the California State Board of Parole Hearings questioned Mark's trade-off with the government that put Jimmy in prison and Meir Itaev back on the street.

"We know this guy's a thug," said Neil Schneider, the presiding commissioner of the Board of Parole Hearings. "He's a Russian Mafia, two-bit punk thug with him and his brothers. They're flipped. They're testifying."

Schneider, a former Sacramento Police captain and adjunct professor in the Administration of Justice Department at Los Rios College in Sacramento, was first appointed to the State Board of Parole Hearings by Governor Jerry Brown in July 2018.

Hearings he has presided over include those for Bobby Beausoleil, a Manson family member who was convicted for the murder of his roommate Gary Hinman.

Beausoleil was convicted largely due to the testimony of Mary Brunner, an accomplice who testified against him in exchange for leniency. Brunner was a Manson girl and the mother of one of the cult leader's sons. On the night of the Sharon Tate killing in October 1969, Brunner was in custody, having been arrested after going on a shopping spree with a stolen credit card at a department store in the San Fernando Valley.

The use of informants is a common law enforcement practice. Jail house informants frequently extract confessions from suspects that are subsequently used at trial to convict, especially when police interrogations have fallen short.

But there is another class of informant—the criminal insider who informs on his partners in crime. Mark Itaev would be one of those.

"Informants are never good people," Schneider said at Jimmy's parole hearing. "I can't call the feds up and tell them anything they need to know. I don't know anything. Right? So, by very definition, uh, confidential informant normally is somebody in the mix, is a horrible person. No credibility whatsoever. And now this guy's testifying, uh, and you don't testify two separate juries, and they throw a bunch of charges if not for him, true or false, if not for him, Mr. Markzitser would still, could still be alive today…"

Bribed witnesses are against the law. What's the difference between a bribed witness and a paid informant?

Attorney Tony Serra, an expert on the topic, gave a brutally honest assessment.

"A bribed witness does it, by definition, for money. Paid informants will do it for money, but they're doing it for something far more precious than money: liberty.

"They will receive leniency sometimes, you know, avoiding twenty years in prison, ten years in prison, five years in prison. Those kinds of rewards adulterate the truth-seeking process. It has contaminated our courts. Informants are infamously perjurious, and the credibility of the entire system is now in doubt.

"This has now spilled over into most, every other kind of case, and so-called white-collar crime is predominantly informant-oriented. They're either testifying or they're supplying information for search warrants. They supply information for wire taps when they're examined. Ultimately, they, for the most part, are not credible, and they're serving their own interests, and they're falsifying.

"You can't get justice in the informant system because you bring motions to have their identity revealed so that you can solve the falsity that underpinned the case. And for ninety-nine percent of the time, and I'm speaking from a lot of experience, they won't reveal them. They'll even, ultimately, if there's a court order to reveal, they'll dismiss the case rather than reveal.

"They are agent provocateurs, they go in, they infiltrate a group, and then they are the ones that create the crime where they have been. But the agent provocateur is the one that really instigates the crime. They're not revealed. It has destroyed the integrity of the system.

"I believe in the jury system. The jury, you know, are ordinary people. They are the conscience of the community, and if given the opportunity, will see through the fabric of deceit.

"Now, there's not only an increase in usage, but also an increase in the category of informants. It's not on decline. It's rapidly accelerating. Let me just give you some of the jargon. There are credible informants, there's non-tested, non-credible informants, there's material informants, there's percipient informants, there's participatory informants, there's informants before the fact and after the fact. We now have more nomenclature in our law for informant and informant activity than any law that has evolved on this planet.

"To answer your question, there is no difference between a bribed witness and a paid informant. Informants may seek money, but often they seek some other benefit, be it for themselves personally or indirectly."

In the case of Mark Itaev, the payment was freedom for his uncle Meir.

Aleks paid for it with his life; Kitlas paid with 20 years in prison. Audrey Lane paid for it by being emotionally traumatized and socially marginalized as a homeless, unwed teen with a high-risk lifestyle.

At the time of this writing, Audrey and her daughter are estranged. She hasn't seen Patrick James Kitlas since he was sentenced to prison.

Kelley Leigh is happily married. She and her husband have earned admirable reputations for their excellent renovation, repair, and creative customization of recreational vehicles.

A contemporary of Jimmy and Audrey during their time on the streets of Hollywood who chose to remain anonymous while helping us with research, despite a significant period in recovery, relapsed into a multi-week period of binge drinking.

Bravely determined to battle the addiction to alcohol that compelled her back to the same streets from which she escaped over a decade ago, she made an appointment to undergo medically assisted detox.

Sadly, she overslept that morning and was turned away at the door because she arrived ten minutes late.

Despite her tearful begging, she was refused treatment and told that this would "teach her a lesson." She had a sudden massive seizure and dropped dead just a few blocks from the clinic near the corner of Pico and La Brea.

"Her dead body was regarded as nothing but sidewalk litter for about five hours before the city came and took it away like so much inconvenient street trash," says Kelley Leigh. "That sounds damn harsh, but that's what I heard. That part of town is not exactly the empathy epicenter of civilization anyway."

Kelley and the boy she called Jimmy haven't seen each other since he got out of prison. He's in the Bay Area; she's in Los Angeles, and there are two decades of life's changes and lifestyles between them.

"He's not a street kid anymore," says Kelley. "He is a mature, spiritual adult—husband and father. He works and I bet he has plans for the future."

Kitlas has true plans for his life and future well-being. The ranch is still there, and Kitlas's daughter is now living on site, being helpful to her aged and loving grandmother.

"My grandfather is gone now too," said Kitlas. "I now have the knowledge and skills to really keep that place up and running, plus take care of my grandmother. I am going to change my parole to Riverside County and my wife and I are gonna get out of the city and get back to where I once belonged." He laughs at his Beatles joke, radiating a positive aura of confidence and clarity.

AFTERWORD

As a reporter, I spent a lot of time with cops working in the field, and when shit went down, the informants, mostly criminals on probation or parole, were usually the first sources for information.

Usually, they're rats, the lowest of the low.

Crooks despise them, cops barely tolerate them. But these guys, Mark and Gary Itaev, are different and don't quite fit the mold that typically applies to informants.

Instead of tolerating them, the cops were using them.

The reasons are varied and somewhat understandable.

Federal officers are under enormous pressure to bring cases to court. That was especially true during the Clinton administration, and the ethos carried over into the early Bush years, or at least until the War on Terror was in full swing.

Unlike movies like *Donnie Brasco*, where a cop goes undercover for months or even years and becomes part of a criminal enterprise like the Mafia, most of the time federal cases are made on informants seeking leniency for themselves or their cohorts.

As for local police, they're tasked with "keeping our streets safe." They can't do it on their own. As we pointed out earlier, street-level sex workers, low-end drug dealers, and even the homeless are pressured to "snitch" on higher ups so that the cops can get information they need to make cases or clean up the corners.

Many times, informants reside in the jails. In our book, *A Taste for Murder*, Burl and I discovered that it was a jailhouse informant who provided key evidence against Angelina Rodriguez, and it ultimately sent her to death row. In another of our books, *Betrayal in Blue*, Burl and I talked to organized crime figures and dirty cops involved in the drug trade in Brooklyn, New York in the 1980s and 1990s. These were tough guys who hated rats and snitches with a passion. This case turns that ethos on its ear.

Court records show that to maintain a criminal enterprise, Mark Itaev traded information with the DEA and other law enforcement agencies on a regular basis. He helped capture competing dope dealers, counterfeiters, thieves, and ultimately turned over the nuts and bolts of a murder case— one in which he was intimately involved, as documented in this book.

I have often thought that this information exchange between Mark, Gary, and their federal handlers was like something pulled from a dim sum menu in a dingy Hong Kong-style restaurant, where ladies stroll the dining area with carts and demand you take steamed buns, vegetables, or fried shrimp before grabbing a card from your table and stamping it with a letter that signifies the item's value.

The transaction that led to Aleks's murder seems somehow like that.

Choose anything from Column A for a minor consideration; Column B for something better; or Column C for a "get out of jail free" card for a relative. It might have been that simple.

We tried on numerous occasions to speak to the Itaev family about this story. Through attorney Kiana Sloan-Hillier, they declined to comment. Burl and I wish we could have included their perspective as well.

In the 1990s, I wrote briefly about the gas tax scam. Fortunately, I saved the federal indictment for 30+ years and only pulled it out when I heard of this case. It led down a rabbit hole that introduced me to Daniel Patterson, a colorful guy with a great memory and some amazing stories.

That rabbit hole also led to Dan Moldea, a seasoned reporter who covered the *Anita Busch v. Anthony Pellecano* case.

Moldea is the author of several great books on the organized crime infiltration of the Reagan White House, the National Football League, and the Teamsters. He has written about Robert F. Kennedy and Jimmy Hoffa, but never formally tackled Russian or Armenian organizations operating in the U.S.

Burl and I thought it would be helpful to include a history of events involving the Russian mob—such as it is—in an appendix to this book. It lends a solid understanding and chronology of events that may have had a butterfly effect on situations and alliances that connect even tangentially to the murder in this book.

We're also including, for your edification, a summary of guidelines regarding confidential informants created when Janet Reno was U.S. Attorney General, which were supposedly in force at the time of this story.

—Frank C. Girardot

PHOTOS

Meir "Mike" Itaev

Young Audrey Lane

Daniel Patterson

Authors Frank Girardot and Burl Barer

Frank J. Hagen

Private Eye Fred Wolfson

Famed L.A. gangster "Mickey" Cohen

Jimmy Kitlas, 2024

Judge Elden Fox

Kelley Leigh, 2024

Mark Itaev

Robert Vesco

Young Jimmy Kitlas prior to going to West Hollywood.

Young Jimmy Kitlas hugging his grandfather.

APPENDIX A

This information comes from a combination of witness testimony, federal and state court records, and newspaper articles. Much of it was published on March 31, 1998, as an appendix in a draft copy of the "Tri-State Joint Soviet-Emigre Organized Crime Project" compiled by researchers at Rutgers University School of Criminal Justice on a grant from the U.S. Department of Justice, National Institute of Justice, and as such is in the public record. We've added context and details where appropriate.

> **January 1, 1981**: Rachmel Dementev. Shot to death by Vladimir Reznikov. Allegedly killed after calling Reznikov an informant.

> **March 3, 1981**: Sheila and Slavi Shaknis. Mother and son shot to death, allegedly because their husband/father failed to repay money owed to other criminals.

> **December 5, 1981**: Yuri Brokhin. Shot to death in his New York City apartment. His wife had been found dead in their bathtub sometime earlier; originally thought a suicide, she may have been murdered.

1982: David Eligolashvili. Allegedly involved in loan-sharking and the sale of stolen Torah scrolls. Murdered.

February 6, 1983: Victor Malinsky. Shot to death in Manhattan.

August 21, 1983: Zurab Minakhishvili. Stabbed to death in the Sadko Restaurant in Brighton Beach, Brooklyn, allegedly by Benjamin Nayfeld during a fight.

December 15, 1983: Ilya Goldstein. Shot five times in Manhattan but survived.

January 24, 1984: Evsei Agron. Self-proclaimed "Russian Godfather," Agron came to the U.S. in 1975 and built a criminal empire in Brighton Beach. Shot in the neck as he exited an underground garage in his Park Slope, Brooklyn building. Survived.

February 28, 1984: Mikhail Tolstonog. Shot to death in a boiler room.

May 4, 1985: Evsei Agron. Shot to death. Assassin fired two bullets into his head as he waited for an elevator in his building.

February 3, 1986: Ilya Zeltzer. Shot to death during a shootout inside a Platinum Energy gas distribution office in Brooklyn. Allegedly shot by Vladimir Reznikov in a dispute over bootleg gas.

March 3, 1986: Shaya Kalikman. Shot to death in a Brighton Beach social club, allegedly by Garik Verbitsky.

April 26, 1986: Oleg Vaksman. Allegedly a mid-level cocaine dealer. Shot to death inside a friend's Brighton Beach apartment.

June 13, 1986: Vladimir Reznikov. Shot to death while getting into his car in front of the Odessa Restaurant in Brighton Beach. Allegedly killed by La Cosa Nostra at the request of Russian criminals involved in bootleg gas scams.

July 25, 1986: Anatoly Rubashkin. Shot to death. His body was found in a lot in Sheepshead Bay, Brooklyn.

April 21, 1987: Garik Verbitsky. Known as "Jerry Razor," suspected of murdering Shaya Kalikman. Shot to death in a Brighton Beach social club.

September 13, 1987: Rosala Elyurina. Stabbed to death.

November 18, 1987: Boris Rubinov. Believed to be a low-level criminal killed over a drug debt. Shot to death in his car.

November 18, 1987: Lev Persits. Allegedly involved in bootleg gas scams. Survived but was paralyzed after being shot in the back.

December 5, 1987: Philip Moskowitz. Friend of Michael Markowitz and involved in bootleg gas scams. Found dead in North Brunswick, New Jersey. His body showed signs of torture prior to death.

October 18, 1988: Gregory Yampolsky. Allegedly killed by Felix Furman.

December 10, 1988: Felix Furman. Shot to death in Brighton Beach by Valery Zlotnikov, from whom Furman was extorting money.

May 2, 1989: Michael Markowitz. Shot to death in a car. Arrested in connection with bootleg gas scams; allegedly killed on orders from La Cosa Nostra to prevent cooperation with police.

May 23, 1990: Abram Khaskin. Found shot to death inside a burning car.

January 14, 1991: Boris Nayfeld. Escaped injury when a bomb placed under his car failed to go off.

February 19, 1991: Jerome Slobotkin. In 1988, Slobotkin testified against Nicodemo Scarfo and associates, claiming to be a victim of a Scarfo protection racket. Shot to death near his Philadelphia home by Antuan Bronshtein.

February 28, 1991: Vladimir Vaynerchuk. Bludgeoned to death in an elevator.

March 3, 1991: Vyacheslav Lyubarsky. Allegedly a member of a Soviet narcotics trafficking group importing heroin via Bangkok, Poland, and Brussels. Shot in the buttocks by an unknown assailant in the hall outside his apartment but survived.

March 20, 1991: David Shuster. Allegedly involved in bootleg gas scams. Shot but survived.

May 11, 1991: Emil Puzyretsky. Mob enforcer known for knife use; involved in bootleg gas scams. Shot to death inside the National Restaurant in Brighton Beach. Gunman used a silencer-equipped handgun, firing twice at close range and several more times after he fell.

May 14, 1991: Monya Elson. Reputed leader of a crime group in counterfeiting, drug trafficking, and other activities. Allegedly involved in the murders of Elbrous Evdoev and the Lyubarskys. Shot in Brighton Beach. This attempt suspected as retaliation for the attempt on Vyacheslav Lyubarsky. Other attempts on Elson are detailed below.

May 22, 1991: Gintas Digry. Shot to death in a car in Brooklyn. A second man, Richardas Vasiliavitchus, was wounded.

June 11, 1991: Moisy Zusim and Leonid Khazanovich. Owner of a West Philadelphia jewelry store and his employee shot to death with semi-automatic weapons during a robbery.

July 27, 1991: Fima Miller. Murdered inside a Brooklyn jewelry store. Alleged associate of Namik Karafov and Fima Laskin.

July 30, 1991: Namik Karafov. Shot to death inside his apartment. Several guns were found at scene, but not the murder weapon.

July 8, 1991 (abducted); August 27, 1991 (body found): Yevgeni Mikhailov. Allegedly involved in jewelry theft and fraud. Abducted in Brooklyn; body found in a lot near Kennedy Airport, New York City. Shot four times in the head.

September 27, 1991: Fima Laskin. Stabbed to death in Munich, Germany.

November 1991: Roman Kegules. Stabbed numerous times. Body found floating in Sheepshead Bay, Brooklyn.

December 15, 1991: Robert Sason. Shot in the hand but recovered.

January 12, 1992: Vyacheslav "Slava" and Vadim Lyubarsky. Father and son shot to death in the hallway outside their Brighton Beach apartment. Ambushed after dinner with Slava's wife, Nellie, who was unharmed. In 1995, Monya Elson and others were charged in federal indictment for these and other murders.

January 21, 1992: Efrim Ostrovsky. Shot to death while exiting his stretch limousine in Queens, NY. Hit allegedly arranged by Alexander Slepinin, who was extorting money from Ostrovsky.

May 8, 1992: Said Amin Moussostov. Former Soviet kick-boxer and reputed member of a violent Chechen crime group. Suspected in the murder of Fima Laskin. Shot to death by two unknown gunmen in the hallway of his home in Palisades Park, New Jersey.

June 5, 1992: Elbrous Evdoev. Alleged involvement in prostitution. Shot in the jaw and back in New York City. Survived.

June 23, 1992: Alexander Slepinin. Allegedly responsible for the death of Efrim Ostrovsky. Shot to death in his car. Shot numerous times in the head and back. Monya Elson and others were charged in a federal indictment.

July 4, 1992: Elbrous Evdoev. Shot in the shoulder and hand in New York City. Told police the shooting was ordered by Monya Elson.

August 26, 1992: Boris Roitman. Thought to be an informant for the police. Shot to death. Body found beside a tennis court in Gravesend, Brooklyn. Shot in the chest and neck.

November 6, 1992: Monya Elson. Shot in the forearm by an unknown assailant in Los Angeles. Driven by Leonyard Kanterkantetes to hospital; treated and released. Two days later, an Armenian trying to bomb Kanterkantetes's car was critically injured by premature detonation.

November 1992: Vladimir Zilbersteyn. Shot in the face and upper body by shotgun pellets from another vehicle while driving in Manhattan. Survived. Allegedly due to dispute with Italian mobsters in bootleg motor fuel tax scams.

January 1, 1993: Vanya Sargsyan. Body found in an industrial area in Lynbrook,

Long Island. Brighton Beach resident shot three times in head, chest, and shoulder with an automatic weapon, allegedly over dispute in trade of colored metals.

March 6, 1993: Elbrous Evdoev. Body found fully dressed and frozen solid in a snow bank at an auto salvage yard in Pine Brook, New Jersey. Shot three times in the head.

March 23, 1993: Lev Gendler. Criminal history included arrests in U.S. and Israel for counterfeiting, extortion, kidnapping, and bank fraud. Found dead in his apartment, shot numerous times in the head and body.

June 10, 1993: Michael Libkin. Shot inside his Manhattan antique store by Peter Gripaldi, a California hitman. Gripaldi used a silencer-equipped automatic handgun, shooting Libkin in the groin. After a struggle, Libkin shot Gripaldi in the chest. Both were hospitalized and released. Gripaldi was later convicted based on a Manhattan DA indictment.

July 1993: Monya Elson. Elson, his wife, and bodyguard Oleg Zapinakmine shot in front of Elson's Brooklyn home by Boris Grigoriev. All were treated in a hospital and released. Attempts stemmed from disputes with other Brighton Beach criminal factions.

September 24, 1993: Oleg Zapinakmine. Shot once in the back and killed by an unknown assailant while checking a flat tire on his car in front of his Brooklyn home.

October 20, 1993: Georgiy Sidropulo. Believed to be part of a Russian and Hispanic narcotics group "T.F." (Together Forever). Shot three times in the shoulder, chest, and jaw while sitting in front of a Brighton Beach café. Survived. Shots fired from a van.

December 2, 1993: Vladimir Beigelman. Reputed major cocaine trafficker with ties to the Cali Cartel and La Cosa Nostra; possibly blamed for losing a large cocaine shipment. Shot to death by two unknown males who fired four shots into his neck, head, and back as he exited a van in Queens, NY. Shooters appeared Hispanic.

January 11, 1994: Alexander Gutman. Shot execution-style at his Philadelphia jewelry store by Northeast Philadelphia resident and Soviet émigré Antuan Bronshtein.

January 12, 1994: Oleg Korataev. Former Soviet boxer and brutal mob enforcer. Shot to death near the Arbat Restaurant in Brighton Beach. Shot in back of head while stepping outside for air at a party.

January 17, 1994: Alexander Levichitz ("Sasha Pinya"). Shot three times in the head near the Arbat Restaurant in Brighton Beach but survived. Allegedly a close friend of Monya Elson.

January 21, 1994: Vladimir Karak. Shot to death.

March 23, 1994: Yanik Megasaev. Body found in a pile of garbage in a wooded area near Shore Parkway in Brooklyn. Shot four times in the chest and face.

June 16, 1994: Alexander Graber. Had lived in Brighton Beach for over a year with alleged ties to local organized crime. Shot along with two other men in Moscow by unknown assailants in a car.

July 11, 1994: Naum and Simeon Raichel. Naum was shot three times in the stomach and chest near the Winter Garden Restaurant in Brighton Beach. On the same day, his brother Simeon was severely beaten in Berlin, Germany. Both survived.

January 18, 1995: Arkady Shvartsman. Shot and killed by two gunmen as he sat in his vehicle during evening rush hour, blocks from the Philadelphia Police Department headquarters. A briefcase with over $10,000 in it was left untouched.

April 20, 1995: Heinrich Barel. Shot in the face but survived.

APPENDIX B

On January 8, 2001, U.S. Attorney General Janet Reno issued new Department of Justice Guidelines Regarding the Use of Confidential Informants.

The purpose of these guidelines is to set policy regarding the use of confidential informants in criminal investigations and prosecutions by all Department of Justice Law Enforcement Agencies and Federal Prosecuting Offices.

These guidelines are mandatory and supersede the Attorney General's Guidelines on the Use of Informants in Domestic Security, Organized Crime, and Other Criminal Investigations (December 15, 1976); the Attorney General's Guidelines on FBI Use of Informants and Confidential Sources (December 2, 1980); Resolution 18 of the Office of Investigative Agency Policies (August 15, 1996); and any other guidelines or policies that are inconsistent with these Guidelines.

The complete document can be found at:

www.justice.gov

and www.aclu.org.

BIBLIOGRAPHY

Associated Press. (2000, December 21). "4 accused of faking lab ties in scheme to illicitly acquire $1.6 million in gold." *The San Diego Union-Tribune*, A-4.

Barer, B., & Boyer, M. (Hosts). (2024, July 11). Snitches: Tony Serra, famed attorney [Audio podcast episode]. In True Crime Uncensored with Burl Barer and Mark Boyer. Spotify. https://creators.spotify.com/pod/profile/burl-barer/episodes/SNITCHES--TONY-SERRA--FAMED-ATTORNEY-e2ltfu5/a-abe5sp9

Board of Parole Hearings. (2023, December 14). *Parole Suitability Hearing In the matter of the Parole Consideration Hearing of: Patrick Kitlas, CDCR Number: F13258.* San Quentin State Prison.

California Department of Justice. (1996). *Organized Crime in California: Annual Report to the California Legislature.* Office of the Attorney General.

CityNewsService. "Gold." *CityNewsService*, 20 Dec. 2000. *LexisNexis*, 21 Oct. 2020.

Favot, S. (2019, August 8). Senate *Russian Mob Hearing_writeup.docx.pdf.*

Ford, L. (2002). Anita Busch. Luke Ford. https://www.lukeford.net/profiles/profiles/anita_busch.htm

Herzog, I., & Marshall, E. D. (2017). *Complaint for Declaratory and Injunctive Relief, Busch v. Federal Bureau of Investigation, Case 2:17-cv-01511* (United States District Court, Central District of California, Western Division).

Journal Staff Report. (2000, December 21). "What Do You Suppose Gave Their Plan Away?" *Providence Journal-Bulletin (Rhode Island).*

Kitlas, Jimmy. Interview by Frank C. Girardot. August 2024. Transcript of Kitlas_recording_1 (transcript).mp3.pdf.

Kitlas, Jimmy. Interview by Frank C. Girardot. August 2024. Transcript of Kitlas_recording_2 (transcript).mp3.pdf.

Kitlas, Jimmy. Interview by Frank C. Girardot. August 2024. Transcript of Kitlas_recording_3 (transcript).mp3.pdf.

New Jersey State Commission of Investigation, New York State Commission of Investigation, New York State Organized Crime Task Force, Pennsylvania Crime Commission, & Rutgers University School of Criminal Justice. (1996). Russian-emigre organized crime in the tri-state area. Tri-State Joint Soviet-Emigre Organized Crime Project. https://nj.gov/sci/pdf/russian.pdf

Patterson, Part i "Saturday at 11-05 A.M." Interview by Frank Girardot. 05 Mar. 2021.

Patterson, Part ii "Saturday at 11-10 A.M." Interview by Frank Girardot. 12 Mar. 2021.

Patterson, Part iii "Saturday at 10-10 A.M." Interview by Frank Girardot. 19 Mar. 2021.

Patterson, Part iv Saturday at 11-10 AM. Interview by Frank Girardot. 19 Mar. 2021.

The Sun Chronicle. "Guilty" in $1.6M scam. (2001, September 5). *The Sun Chronicle.* https://www.thesunchronicle.com/guilty-in-1-6m-scam/article_37c3a5b3-e95e-5c77-a299-0898d5de6d3b.html

United States District Court, Central District of California. (2017, April 19). *Plea Agreement for Defendant Mark Itaev* (Case No. 2:16-cr-00140-FMO, Document 84).

United States District Court, Central District of California. (2002, March 19). *Order Modifying Conditions of Bond for Defendant Meir Itaev*. Case 2:01-cr-01295-AHM, Document 60.

United States. Congress. Senate. Committee on Governmental Affairs. Permanent Subcommittee on Investigations. (1996). *Russian organized crime in the United States: Hearing before the Permanent Subcommittee on Investigations of the Committee on Governmental Affairs, United States Senate, One Hundred Fourth Congress, second session, May 15, 1996*. U.S. Government Printing Office.

United States District Court, S.D. New York. (1997, June 16). *U.S. v. Elson*, 968 F. Supp. 900 (S.D.NY. 1997).

United States District Court, Central District of California - Western Division. (2017, July 18). *United States of America v. Mark Vincent Norman* (Case No. CR-16-00140-FMO). Reporter's Transcript of Trial Proceedings.

United States District Court, Central District of California. (2005). *Criminal Minutes—Sentencing and Judgment, United States of America vs. Meir Itaev* (Case No. CR 01-1175-TJH & CR 01-1295(B)-TJH).

United States District Court, Central District of California. (2012, October 30). *Reporter's Transcript of Proceedings, Evidentiary Hearing, Patrick James Kitlas v. F. B. Haws, Case No. CV 08-6651-CW* (Document 47).

United States District Court, Central District of California. (2016, March 11). *United States of America v. Mark Itaev, Yelena Itaev, Dmitri Kocharian, and Mark Vincent Norman: Indictment* (Case No. 16-CR16-0140).

United States District Court for the Central District of California. (2002, October 30). *Second Superseding Indictment: United States of America v. Meir Itaev, Aleksandr Drabkin, and Daniel C. Patterson* (CR 01-1295 (B) - ALM).

United States District Court, Central District of California. (2006, February 15). *Third Superseding Indictment, United States of America v. Anthony Pellicano et al.* (Case No. 05-1046 (C)-RMT).

United States District Court, Central District of California. (2005). *Judgment and Probation/Commitment Order, USA v. Meir Itaev* (Docket No. CR 01-1175-TJH and CR 01-1295(B)-TJH).

Winton, R. (2000, December 23). "Gold Theft Scheme and Earlier Plot May Be Linked, Police Say." *Los Angeles Times*. https://www.latimes.com/archives/la-xpm-2000-dec-23-me-3997-story.html

For More News About Burl Barer and Frank C. Girardot Jr, Signup For Our Newsletter:

http://wbp.bz/newsletter

Word-of-mouth is critical to an author's long-term success. If you appreciated this book please leave a review on the Amazon sales page:

http://wbp.bz/wheremurderliesr

JOHN HINCKLEY JR.: WHO I REALLY AM
https://wbp.bz/johnhinckleyjr

**ALSO AVAILABLE FROM WILDBLUE PRESS,
BURL BARER AND FRANK C. GIRARDOT JR.**

A TASTE FOR MURDER
https://wbp.bz/atfma